HOW TO PROMOTE
That Book You Wrote
A Self-Publishing Guide

Ann Doolan-Fox

© Copyright 2022 Celtic Road Home. All Rights Reserved.

HOW TO PROMOTE That Book You Wrote
A Self-Publishing Guide
Ann Doolan-Fox

Table of Contents
Introduction

Part 1: Book Completion
Chapter One: Now, where did I put that manuscript?
Chapter Two: Believe in your story
Chapter Three: The small stuff (editing) really matters
Chapter Four: What's in a title?

Part 2: Getting published
Chapter One: You Can Judge a book by its cover
Chapter Two: Setting up ISBNs and Barcodes
Chapter Three: Book format, genre, metadata
Chapter Four: Upload book files for publishing

Part 3: Let the Promotions begin
Chapter One: How and where to start?
Chapter Two: How to get noticed online
Chapter Three: All about that Ego
Chapter Four: Slow and Steady wins the race
Chapter Five: Never give up

Part 4: My Journey: Tales from a self-published author
Chapter One: Celtic Road Home to America
Chapter Two: Starting out local
Chapter Three: Homeward (Dublin) bound
Chapter Four: Getting to know Colorful Colorado
Chapter Five: Onwards and Upwards
Chapter Six: Reflections: What I have learned

Epilogue
About the author
Review request

Dedicated to all literary souls brave enough to explore the complex, yet fulfilling world of self-publishing. May the road rise to meet with you at each and every turn...

INTRODUCTION

Have you ever dreamt of one day composing your very own book, even got off to a flying start only to bury it away, for it never again to see the light of day? Wherever those well-intended plans may have strayed, the time has now come to make good on them. While most of us start out all gung-ho on the launch of new and exciting projects; their completion however often turns into an uphill battle. In today's hectic world full of constant outside distractions; it becomes so much easier said than done. As a writer, you owe it to yourself to carve out that very special time towards establishing a creative writing schedule. Find yourself that quiet sanctuary space where you can settle into a comfortable routine and the words will soon begin to flow. Before you even realize what's happening, pages will develop into chapters, paving the way towards your becoming a self-published author.

The sole purpose in my compiling this guide book centers on motivating you towards completion of your Beloved written project. Far from a professional writer by any means, I feel honored to help guide you through the complex maze of all that pertains to the self-publishing world. There will certainly be moments when you may find the undertaking proves too much of a challenge. Always remind yourself though, that anything hard in Life is always worthwhile in the end. If I managed to do it, so can you while possibly achieving even more incredible outcomes? Who in the world wants to live Life with memories of "maybe's" and "what if's"? Why not give it a chance; what do you have to lose?

Besides the necessary editing chores, selecting fonts, formats, title, and book cover design et al., get ready for an exhilarating adventure of constant twists and turns. Over the past decade, with the introduction of the self-publishing market (Amazon, Kobo, IngramSpark, Lulu, Smashwords, etc.) the process has become so much easier for aspiring authors like you and me. Make today the day to recreate that manuscript (begun some time ago) by transforming it into an artistic masterpiece. I will show you how to get started, from allocating your book ISBN number, barcode, through the

Part One: Book Completion

editing process and on to book self-publishing sites. Finally, let's get you promoting and marketing that future published literary work of art.

How you choose to promote your book will depend entirely on you. From personal experience, I recommend the more dedicated time and energy you devote will continually reap future rewards, both in financial and spiritual ways. Ego can play a huge role throughout this process, with upcoming positive and negative reviews on your horizon. However, with the passing of time, you will surely adapt either by choosing to take them personally or not. Bear in mind, the more you put yourself out in the world; the more those new readers will gravitate towards your book. In conclusion, by giving it your all and nothing less, you can never fail. How will you ever know unless you try? What if you fly?

The final part of this useful guide book includes a compilation of personal stories/experiences on promoting my first book called: **"Celtic Road Home: A Memoir"** All events take place beginning in early 2017 through 2019 across the beautiful state of Colorado. There is even a surprise visit back to my childhood hometown of Dublin, Ireland.

My sincere wish for you is to not only gain valuable tips along the way, but most importantly feel confidence in venturing outside of your comfort zone. The journey ahead will undoubtedly include both smooth and rocky roads, but those less travelled will always end up the most memorable ones. You alone, hold the key to converting your words into an upcoming first edition. I wish you all the very Best of Celtic Luck in all future endeavors along this fun and exciting new book adventure...

"May the roads rise to meet you and may the wind be always at your back."

Happy writing! How To Promote That Book You Wrote is divided into four separate parts:

1. Book Completion
2. Getting Published
3. Let the Promotions Begin
4. My Journey: Tales from a self-published author

Part One: Book Completion
Chapter 1: Now where did I put that manuscript?

"Optimism is the faith that leads to achievement. Nothing can be done without hope and confidence."
- Helen Keller

Our addictive and interactive world with its own stressors, often robs us of any sense of daily accomplishments. What, if any spare time is left to work on that book you first began a month, a year or even a decade ago? Okay, there are no more excuses; you now recognize your written work was the beginning of something extraordinary. Why not make today the perfect time to get back into your writing groove once more?

It's a beautiful day, so what better time than right now to rescue that dusty, worn and abandoned manuscript. Now, where did you last place those inspiring pages/saved computer files? Let's look for them….you know they're nearby, just waiting to be rescued at last. What was that; you don't have the time or energy? Oh yes you most certainly do! Imagine that special moment upon rediscovery of those long forgotten pages. This is just the beginning of a self-fulfilling path towards your future recognition as a published author. The adventure and highlight of a lifetime awaits…..so, what are you waiting for?

Let's begin the process at a slow pace by rereading your precious written work as you will get to review it with a fresh pair of eyes. Although, an initial reaction to edit will begin to kick in, allow some time to ease back into your unique writing flow. Bear in mind, most renowned writers have reedited their work multiple times

Part One: Book Completion 7

over before ever reaching an acceptable resolution. Also, remember you are never alone on this chosen literary path but have now joined an elite club of aspiring authors around the globe. One day in the not too distant future, you will feel immense pride whenever referred to as a "published author". All of that dedicated hard work will start to pay off, leaving you with a lifetime memory of achievement.

Did you know that on average, a first time author will dedicate anywhere from four months to an entire year on the creation of their book from start to finish? Such a timeline will also reflect upon your chosen book genre, dedicated writing routine, as well as relevant research. To ensure the process is a smoother one, why not set yourself a regular, realistic and attainable writing goal? Picture yourself answering to a demanding boss who allocates you a daily, weekly or monthly work deadline. Be sure to reward yourself for each achieved accomplishment along the way. You might estimate a weekly minimum word amount, while making separate notes to help monitor ongoing progress.

As you slowly compile chapter by chapter, feel free to seek additional help along the way towards that publishing deadline. Online engines such as Google, YouTube etc. can help with multiple avenues yet to be pursued. Advance at your own pace without allowing information overload to overwhelm your mind. Doesn't time just fly whenever you happen to be online researching any given subject? Make sure to take plenty of notes along the way as you organize and customize your book outline. To avoid confusion, it can be useful to create new file categories as you share related book articles to your mail inbox. This pertinent information really comes in handy at a later date, thus saving much valuable time.

Take into account new writers will typically devote a few days a week, often composing @ 1500 words equivalent to three or four book pages. Obviously, some days might account for more or less, depending on your own personal routine. Family, work, health etc. can all play a major role towards the time management of your writing habits. Be kind to yourself and your loved ones throughout this process by allocating equal quality time and energies to all. A talented artist once confided in me on how she loved rising each day at the crack of dawn. Turns out those few precious hours of solitude ignited her creative motivation towards new and exciting art pieces. Even with a busy lifestyle, you can always create quiet time for your written project. As a gentle reminder; only you can make it happen.

     Setting a regular routine will soon turn into a highly-talented skill as you carve out your creative, writing schedule. Dressed in comfortable clothing, with a nice mug of tea/coffee at your side, discover that quiet escape in your home where you get to release your inner author soul. Stay in the moment as you begin to transfer your deep thoughts and ideas into the written word. If today is not cutting it, let it be and go for a walk, watch TV, listen to music, people watch at a café etc. Only write when you feel inspired to do so as this will create your best work. Remember writing is the journey with your book becoming your destination. Take whatever breaks necessary that might replenish your writing ability during this entire process with you being the ultimate keeper of your story.

     The famous American author Ernest Hemingway, a notorious late night drinker, would often rise before dawn to write, stating: "There is no one to disturb you and it is cool or cold and you come to your work and warm as you write. Stop when you know what is going to happen next." In a 1958 interview with the Paris Review he added: "You write until you come to a place where you still have your juice and know what will happen next and you stop and try to live through until the next day when you hit it again."

Part One: Book Completion

Helpful hints to motivate writing on a regular basis:
1. Find your perfect/comfortable/private writing space
2. Create a writing routine to suit your schedule
3. Set yourself attainable daily/weekly writing goals with end rewards
4. Act as though you are already a professional author
5. Remain open to new ideas/characters for upcoming chapters
6. Keep tips, notebooks and story lines close by for referral
7. Take time away to refresh your mind
8. Perform a quick edit at the end of each chapter
9. Allow feedback from family & friends to help feed your writing energy
10. Practice makes Perfect
11. Have Confidence in you/your written work

Time away from your writing routine can prove most beneficial in so many aspects. First of all, a walk/hike in the fresh air will not only add oxygen but also stimulate your brain with fresh ideas and prevent brain fog. Did you know that the Victorian English fiction author, Charles Dickens would routinely walk as many as twenty miles a day noting: "If I could not walk far and fast, I think I should just explode and perish."? Although twenty miles might be a stretch; any outside time, even just a brisk walk just might do the trick to get you back on the writing track.

November is **NATIONAL WRITING MONTH** and geared towards new/existing authors to write a 50,000 word novel between the 1st and 30th of the month. **NaNoWriMo** began as a challenge between friends in 1999 and has today grown into a global event with hundreds of thousands participating each year. Perhaps the month of November would be the perfect starting point to writing your book. It's as good a month as any, right?

Take into account, the total page numbers in an average book can range anywhere from two to around four hundred. As words flow into sentences on the screen, your story soon begins to take shape. On days where it may seem impossible to get those creative juices flowing, don't fret, as there will be many better days ahead. Before your very eyes, pages will accumulate and voila…you are on a roll. On those productive days, go ahead and reward yourself with a favorite treat; you have certainly earned it.

To add some extra perspective on book length; the average fiction novel consists of about 90,000 words (300 book pages) while a non-fiction version will typically hold some 75,000 words (275 book pages). 250 words per page is the general norm for most printed materials. You can always take a look at book lengths on several online platforms or at your local library/bookstore to estimate similar volumes among your selected genre/s.
While in the course of writing your book, remember this valuable tip: have your book long enough to tell your story but short enough to hold your future reader's attention. Although this may seem tricky as you settle into a writing groove, there are always ways to keep it appealing. When you feel ready to share your heartfelt words, perhaps at a chapter's end, allow people you trust to read and review your written work. Taking advantage of this valuable feedback will serve as a critical and helpful guide going forward. Try to avoid taking negative comments personally but instead use them as well-meaning constructive advice. Never allow an outside source to persuade the altering of your storyline. After all, this is your baby and nobody but you gets to chart its course.

Another area for improvement of your writing ability may lie even closer than you think. Have you looked into any writing groups in your local area? I will

Part One: Book Completion 11

bet you are unaware most public libraries host writing groups who meet up regularly for brainstorming sessions. Bouncing off ideas and opinions with other aspiring writers can prove invigorating and may even help you to discover a consistent writing routine. Listening to stories also provides accountability while setting new attainable goals. Some members may have already self-published their books, thereby offering their own expertise. Without committing to any one group, you might even relish the uniqueness and camaraderie of like-minded and creative fellow authors like you.

Maintain the editing of your work to a minimum as it can distract you from your creative writing flow. This way, you will feel less likely to aim for perfection; you know it doesn't exist. Each time you finish writing for the day, feel free to perform a brief edit. Towards the end of each chapter, you can always give it a more thorough revision. Such a routine will help reduce the major edit at book completion. Most helpful of all; try to read the entire chapter out loud, preferably to another listener. Reading it aloud will detect not only simple grammatical errors along the way but also alert you to a lyrical flow. If, in the future, should you wish to create an audible format/version, you will hear how it sounds to the listener.

Have you managed to settle into your writing flow yet? Not to worry; some authors take a while to achieve a regular writing routine. In the meantime, here are some useful tips to consider:
1. Choose your own individual writing style. Are you speaking in 1st, 2nd or 3rd person?
2. Have something special you would like the reader to hear
3. Keep your sentences/paragraphs shorter in length
4. Try to avoid big, fluffy vocabulary
5. Start small and build the storyline as you go
6. Stay consistent with your original book outline

7. A sense of humor is always welcome
8. Begin and end each chapter drawing in the reader
9. Is this a book that you would love to read/buy? Why?

If you would rather compose your manuscript in longhand, know you are not alone. JK Rowling regularly begins each new project in hand-written format, later transferring it to the computer. Can you imagine, she first began writing stories inside notebooks in cozy Scottish neighborhood cafes while her infant daughter slept in a stroller nearby? At the time, she and her offspring were surviving on government benefits. Today, she has since sold more than 450 million books worldwide. If this story doesn't "Inspire" you, what will?

Know that there are many authors out there, (like readers) who find the shuffling of physical paper highly satisfying throughout the writing process. If you lack the ability to type quickly; composing the old-fashioned way just might be for you. Thoughts might flow at a faster rate and you can always copy your pages to a screen at a later time. Whichever format suits you the best will secure your comfort zone as a writer. Have fun with each new writing experience and rest in the knowledge you will eventually find your way…

"Success is the sum of small efforts – repeated day in and day out."
-Robert Collier

Part One: Book Completion
Chapter 2: Believe in your story

"The future belongs to those who believe in the beauty of their dreams."
- Eleanor Roosevelt

Throughout the years, have family and friends often admired your unique way with words and natural abilities in storytelling? As a youngster, were you gifted with a vivid imagination, forever inventing fantasy stories from the routines of everyday life? During school days, perhaps some of your stories were read aloud by the teacher? Did classmates ask for help with their English homework? Whatever the case, the time has now come to acknowledge those lost writing talents by launching your story out there for the world to read...

Let's travel back in time to recapture the feeling of why you first began to write, while paving the way forward into your becoming a published author.

Self-confidence in your written work begins from deep within, making it crucial to staying true to your craft from start to finish. Moments of doubt will always come and go to test your abilities, but it's up to you to push forward regardless. No one else can compose your unique story but you, so allow that intuitive strength to become your armor. Let the ups and downs of self-reflection fade away as your storyline comes together word by word.

You are not alone as all authors struggle with self-doubt from time to time, often succumbing to author's block. Negative thoughts have a knack of creeping in during the writing process which is to be expected. However, remind yourself of all the wonderful readers out there yet to savor that future book of yours. Keep the faith that your contribution is unique and who knows where it might end up around the globe.

Stephen King composed his debut novel "Carrie" while employed as a high school English teacher in Maine. One day in 1971, while grading student test papers, he began to dabble in his future writing career. Disillusioned with the first three pages, he threw them in the trash, only to be retrieved by his wife Tabitha. Just two short years later, the movie of the same title was released, becoming a box office hit. On a side note, who is to say that your book might also someday turn into a successful movie? How will you ever know unless you try...?

The research of other successful writers within your genre/category may prove helpful not only towards honing your craft, but also on the creation of a stand out book. Focus on how you would like the reader to feel, browsing your work as if you were reading it with a critical mind. Do you look forward to the next paragraph, page and chapter? If the answer is yes; you are definitely on the right track. Placing yourself on the outside looking in can really elevate your writing towards targeting the bold expectations of future readers.

There remains such solitude in writing which at times, can bring the author to a dark place of worthlessness. Here is where belief and commitment to your work begins to take hold. As pages magically appear before your very eyes, it enhances that inner ability to inch closer towards your literary goal. The process might include finishing up a short story/collection, writing 500 words at a time, or even self-publishing your first book. Whatever the case may be, write only when you are feeling inspired to do so as this will most likely create some of your best work. It is not necessary to compare yourself to an established author like Stephen King, writing three pages a day. But do believe in your own individual writing style while establishing your craft along the way. As you go, a routine will soon materialize,

Part One: Book Completion

making writing practice a breeze.

Embrace those days when you feel most positive about your work as they help guide you onwards and upwards. Always stay true to yourself as the reader may notice any minor changes in your writing style. As chapters are pieced together, the main storyline will begin to take shape forming the outline of your very first book. Who knows, this may be the first of a future book series following rave reviews.

In today's world, you can share your written work in a myriad of ways on social media, email or even via a personal blog. Building a support system of feedback throughout the writing process will only further boost your confidence, discarding those thoughts of not feeling good enough…. Just know that you already are. Potential readers are out there, waiting in the wings to revel in your hidden writing talents.

Would you believe me if I told you there are millions of potential writers out there who lack the confidence, valuable time or will to write a book like you are doing right now? It takes incredible courage to follow your heart, commit to the entire ordeal of book-writing and following through until the end. One day in the very near future, the fruits of your hard labor will be realized as you cradle your first physical book in your hands. What an incredible feeling that will turn out to be.

In the meantime, as you ease into your own personalized writing style, do not allow your confidence to be thwarted by self-criticism by comparing your work to fellow authors. You may even reflect: "Is this writing a waste of time? Will anyone bother to read my book? Should I be doing something else?" Ask yourself why you first began writing this book and relive that special moment. It will only serve as additional writing motivation along the way to becoming self-published.

Now, let's get back to that amazing book you're working on, shall we? How far along are you? Is it a book of poetry, non-fiction, the beginning of a crime or fantasy series? Perhaps you are putting together a self-help guide following the world plandemic that we have all had to endure for the last while. Good on you for making the decision to follow through on your literary pursuit. Believe you have a great story to tell that will not only let the reader in, but will also make them smile, laugh, cry, while always wanting more. You will never discover the number of readers worldwide your book has touched. This knowledge alone should Inspire your journey forward.

To help guide **Believing** in your very own story, take time to take a break and read a book/s in a similar genre. Observing fellow authors might instill new ideas on how your own story line is developing. You might feel inspired or decide on what to avoid as you proceed towards the next chapter, etc. Watch a YouTube video on other writers in a similar situation, while taking notes of helpful tips. All writers are uniquely individual; you will soon discover innovative ways that will work best for you. You just never know unless you keep pushing forwards.

Today might have brought you to a standstill, perhaps with a touch of writer's block, so here's what we are going to do about that:

Stepping Aside for a time period is going to help you feel refreshed upon your return either later in the day or tomorrow. Your mind will feel so much clearer after the release of any negative energy. Slow down and just Breathe….there's no rush to get your book written today.

Winds of Change will arise from participation of the following leisure activities: escaping outdoors, going to the movies, reading a book, people-watching at an indoor/outside café, catching up with a friend, shopping, browsing at a library/bookstore, volunteering, helping a friend, etc. Observing (not eavesdropping) on everyday conversations just might introduce new ideas or book characters not yet developed. See what those little writing breaks can do?

Part One: Book Completion 17

    Upon your return, you may manifest renewed confidence in your writing skills, come up with ideas for a new character, change direction in your story for the better, or even perhaps catch a few undetected corrections. Most importantly, you will feel renewed energy. This new Positive thinking will only help to create an innovative reading experience. Therefore, make sure to take any necessary time outs to further enhance your writing skills as often as you would like. One day in the future, you will be so glad you did.

    Only ever write when feeling inspired and ready, as your creativity will always be plentiful during this special time. Always remember that authors the world over have all at times suffered feelings of self-worth but rallied back around and got their works published. Not one single author has ever had the perfect manuscript to offer their publisher, without having to perform a ton of rewrites, edits and the like. So whenever you're feeling discouraged, think of all the millions of authors out there whose club you have now joined and know you are all on this literary path as one. If writing comes naturally, you will just write and write until you get tired and worry about the editing stuff at a later stage. Quantity will eventually turn into quality so just have fun with it and witness reality turning into magic and believe me, it will.

    According to information from Medium.com, the following is an interesting list of additional professions from famous authors:
- Ernest Hemingway was an ambulance driver, journalist, big game hunter and war correspondent
- Stephen King was a janitor, English teacher and commercial laundry worker.
- Harper Lee worked in the airline industry
- Octavia Butler was a potato chip inspector
- Douglas Adams was a bodyguard

    The message here is that you never know where your hard work, sitting at a computer, tablet or writing pad is going to take you along your journey. Believe you can and you will succeed. If everyone decided to give up writing, there would never be reading materials to help inspire, inform, teach, stimulate, guide and entertain us ever again. From a reader's perspective, books represent a huge range of emotions, imagination, knowledge etc. but above all, a place where we can escape to for a limited time. The world is big and varied enough for your writing talents to affect those future readers who are just awaiting your book's availability.

    Even before the world shutdown, the United States held an average of 1.7 million self-published books in 2018 alone. Consider that revised number today and it might be double with an over abundance of aspiring home-bound writers. Now, more than ever before, you are sure to be among those other millions of first-time authors so let's make this book a memorable one, shall we? Timing will be perfect whenever you feel ready and inspired to follow that inner voice. Today may be the perfect moment you have been waiting for; let's do this.

    An interesting story for you; a UK team of palliative care nurses conducted a study some years ago of elderly patients before passing away. It was noted that almost half of them had lived with regret on not having pursued past Life dreams. If only given the chance again….The Life lesson here is to always follow your heart, jump into the pool at the deep end and take that chance. How will you ever know unless you leave your comfort zone, if only for a while? Upon writing my first book, Karen, a dear lifelong friend offered this valuable advice: "What if I try? What if I fly?" The same goes for you…Are you ready to take this leap?

    Throughout your dedicated writing, as long as you stay focused on your end goal, you can never go wrong. As an end note, always take a break from your book to ensure feeling refreshed on your return. Remember someday, you too are "gonna

Part One: Book Completion

be old" upon reflection of your life achievements. Wouldn't it be wonderful to feel such immense pride on having followed through on this one goal...writing and publishing your book, exclaiming: "YES, I did it!"

"There is nothing like a dream to create the future."
- Victor Hugo

Part One: Book Completion
Chapter 3: Why the small stuff really matters (Editing)

"Over every mountain there is a path, although it may not be seen from the valley."
- Theodore Roosevelt

Congratulations on reaching the finishing stages of your beloved book and welcome to the mundane world of self-editing. Although it may seem like an endless task of constant edits, page corrections etc., I can promise you ongoing satisfaction upon completion. This is your final opportunity to make your book sparkle from start to finish, offering a superior presentation to the future reading world. Most importantly, remember the essence of editing should always result in an overall book review without ever rewriting your story.

*It is vital to utilize all the resources required in editing your book. Set your own pace while correcting grammar, spelling etc. and scan a paragraph or a page at a time until the very last word.

Before the editing process begins, consider these crucial tips:
1. Make sure to save every little edit as you go – prevents extra work later
2. Keep a notebook by your side at all times – will help to maintain sanity
3. No need to over edit – change the book outline/theme
4. Read aloud each chapter – gives overall context/tone/accuracy
5. Take full advantage of free online editing assistance
6. Be content with the final edit – no need to strive for perfection

First of all, send all your book files to a local printing service which will result in a much cheaper/less

Part One: Book Completion   21

stressful option. Once you have proudly scanned through that thick bundle of papers, set your manuscript aside for at least a week or more. This necessary pause will allow time for your written work to settle (like a fine wine) before the editing process can commence.

As your book rests, use this down time to browse the works of fellow authors in your chosen genre for perspective on your own written word. Did you come across writing and spelling errors? What emotions did the book conjure up? How does your writing style compare? Were the chapters organized in the right places? Did you look forward to the next one? Would you have made any changes? Was it unique and did you enjoy the read? Does the writer stay in the weeds (overuse of flowery language etc.) too much? All these questions and ideas will help pave the way towards a more thorough book editing experience, keeping you mindful of additional corrections/changes.

The very first draft of your book is complete once you have come to an acceptable ending. It will take a minimum of three additional edits before you begin uploading finalized book files to self-publishing platforms etc. Have you run a complete spell-check yet? This would be a good time to do so as it will decrease those annoying spelling/grammatical errors that accumulate over time.

The Relevance of Three book edits:
1. 1st edit reviews initial storyline, flow, grammar, punctuation etc.
2. 2nd edit is more thorough: language, corrections/sentence changes
3. Final and most extensive revision.

*In addition, read the entire book out loud three times.

Take into account that a professional editor would have decided in the opening paragraphs alone as to whether your book makes the publishing cut or not. Allow that to serve as a critical guide along the editing path by imagining your worst critic's viewpoint at every turn. It also helps to accumulate additional feedback from trusted family and friends who read books on a regular basis. Hiring a professional proofreader/book editor to revise your work does not come cheap. You could spend anywhere from a few hundred dollars and more depending on experience.

    The role of a book editor involves correcting core writing issues such as sentence construction, clarity of language, narrative, story/chapter sequence, style, tone as well as the overall gist of the book. A proofreader comes in after the final edit is complete and searches for misspelled words, incorrect punctuation along with textual/numerical inconsistencies etc. If you set your mind to it, you alone can undertake all this work, taking your time and not rushing through to get it done all at once. They say: "Patience is a virtue" and it will certainly test you throughout this editing ordeal but also remember: "Where there's a will, there's a way".

    Take full advantage of the multiple free online platforms to upload your files from Word etc. to sites such as Grammarly, Ginger, Paper Rater, White Smoke and many others. An additional spell check will also prove beneficial as a final overview of your work. For an added price, many sites offer more extensive editing such as sentence format, vocabulary suggestions, word repetition or even whether you are plagiarizing an author. Of course, this decision will depend on your comfort level and budget, but it might help to have an extra independent opinion.

    *At the beginning of each new chapter, make sure the <u>opening paragraph is not indented</u>. You can indent every other paragraph by a half inch (hitting the tab will work). Also, remove double spaces at the end of sentences; a single space will suffice. The majority of editors and publishing houses generally use the industry standard of 1.5 line double-spacing when printing books.

Part One: Book Completion

However, it is always wise to double check the publishing site's requirements at the formatting stage.

Remember back in school when that essay you took such pride in was returned emblazoned with red ink? Chances are misspellings/incorrect grammar was often the culprit. Take extra care while implementing some of the following homophonic words commonly misspelt by all of us:

It's/its, there/they're/their, affect/effect, accept/except, further/farther, who/whom, lay/lie, aloud/allowed, capital/capitol, your/you're, then/than, into/in to, good/well, whether/weather, complement/compliment, principal/principle, stationary/stationery, wear/where, etc.

The overall editing process will surpass corrections of all errors, eliminate unnecessary vocabulary, alter the writing tone, modify suitable language for the selected genre, clarify theme/message and polish up/meet specific final word count.

Take for example; in the professional world of editing, there are several facets of the editing process:
1. Developmental editing: Does the story align with the genre?
2. Structural editing: Is the message communicated to the reader?
3. Content editing: How does the book flow?
4. Line editing: Focuses on style/use of language
5. Copy editing: Microscopic correction of grammar, spelling etc.
6. Fact checking: Revision of quotes, slang, dates, events etc.
7. Proofreading: Final preparation with complete book review

The reading of your entire book out loud to yourself and others will be beneficial in a number of ways. Place yourself in the shoes of the reader and imagine you are

creating an audio book version (who knows what the future may hold?) while listening to the overall tone.
- How does the general storyline unfold?
- Is the introduction too short/long?
- Do you like how the book sounds/direction it takes?
- Are you immersed in the theme from beginning to end?
- Does it sound grammatically correct?
- Are there repetitive phrases throughout?
- Are there too many unnecessary flowery words?
- Are there excessive I, me and my's (memoir)?

When you incorporate reading aloud as part of your overall editing, you are bound to end up with a more complete and polished book. Future readers will also notice the difference as it will flow much better.

For the most part, authors of fiction and non-fiction books will edit in similar ways with a few exceptions: Possible Fiction edits:
- Is the main character introduced in chapter one?
- Are additional protagonists introduced too quickly?
- Does the storyline have a good pace?
- Are there vivid descriptions that draw the reader in?
- Is there too much dialogue?
- Avoid over usage of words like said/asked etc.
- Keep the plot interesting/the reader guessing?

The overall editing process of all book types will undoubtedly involve countless hours of corrections as well as a keen attention to every minor detail. This may be the hardest work you have done so far despite having written an amazing book. Just remember, you won't be editing forever and will ultimately reach a moment of incredible achievement and pride. "If a thing is worth doing, it's worth doing well." (proverb).

At any time during the editing phase, should you become overwhelmed by it all; the assistance of a professional can help. Before that step however, take another quick look at some general reminders:

Part One: Book Completion

- Does the theme remain consistently captivating throughout?
- Have all the spelling and grammatical errors been corrected?
- Would I read/buy this book?

    Once you feel no additional corrections are deemed necessary, go ahead and perform one final spell check. Reviewing your work as you write lessens the workload during the final book edits. Once again, if you perform a brief edit/revision following each chapter, it will avoid that major redo upon your book's completion. You can also print out chapters as you write, making it easier to catch mistakes/sentence formats. Each individual writer will find/master their own unique writing habits/quirks that will guide the way forward.

    Taking full advantage of time-consuming research can only further enhance/strengthen your writing skills. With dedicated effort, you can transform your undrafted edit into a polished literary work of art.

    In the end, don't be so hard on yourself and remember no writer is perfect and Rome wasn't built in a day. When was the last time you read a book from one of your favorite authors? Although it may have exuded a professional appearance, I bet there were more than a few typo's throughout the entire read. Now that you have conquered the editing process, you will easily detect errors on all future reading materials. Hey, perhaps there's a surprise career for you ahead as a proof reader.

"Make today your masterpiece."
                                                         –John Wooden

Part One: Book Completion
Chapter 4: What's in a title?

"Success only comes to those who dare to attempt."

-Mallika Tripathi

Well done on arriving at this exciting moment of choosing a title for your beloved book. Did you know your title and cover will go hand in hand towards attracting all those future readers? The number one marketing strategy for any author includes designated choices of book title and cover respectively.

Have you already decided on a final title? Is it a catchy one that captures the essence of your storyline? It would definitely be worthwhile checking on whether a duplicate title exists to maintain your book's uniqueness. Do a search via Amazon etc. as well as TESS, a Trademark Electronic Search System (US) at www.uspto.gov Should you plan a series of books, this site will also allow you to apply for a trademark. However, it is not optional with one book alone. Registering for a trademark can become a complex task, often requiring the assistance of a property intellectual attorney.

Feel free to use an online book generator tool to search for a duplicate title which will narrow down your selected book title. Should a duplicate exist, you may wish to create a more original one to avoid competing with another author. This is the perfect moment to make your title a memorable one. A stand out title that is both bold and beautiful can mean the difference between an eventual sale or not. Testing a series of multiple titles among family, friends and fellow avid readers will help you determine a final informed decision. A voting procedure using a process of elimination might also

Part One: Book Completion

present you with your winning title. Who knows, with all that additional input; you just might find the perfect one. Don't forget to reward those who have helped you along the way.

Titles do not generally include copyrights, thereby allowing you the opportunity to make your title an eye-catching one. A copyright does not protect a book title but will protect you as the sole author of your book and its contents.

An important factor towards creating the perfect book title will be based upon familiarity with your target audience and their chosen genre. An unforgettable title is one that flows, is easily repeated among readers yet transcends beyond the beginning storyline/plot. Neither too short nor too long but rolls off the tongue.

Before you are presented with all the title possibilities, play around with keywords that perfectly describe the contents of your book. Look up the most common ones used in book titles. Which popular book titles tend to achieve the highest rankings in sales/reviews? In order to influence your upcoming book's positioning among search results, the selection of target keywords will play a significant role.

Take into consideration some of the following unique book titles and decide whether the words used tempt you into wanting to read more.

- The Devil Wears Prada
- Are You There, Vodka?
- Everything I Never Told You
- Cloudy With A Chance Of Meatballs
- Love In The Time Of Cholera
- A Time To Kill
- The Art of the Deal/Comeback
- In Cold Blood
- Breaking Dawn
- The Lovely Bones
- I Know Why the Caged Bird Sings

How did each title make you feel? Did you have the impulse to further search either online or via your local library? Place yourself in the shoes of your potential reader, asking the following: Would I find this book interesting enough to read/buy/recommend? Voila, you are on your way to a formidable title.

Keep in mind if you feel your title is not appealing enough to readers/generating sales; you can always change it at anytime. Along with revised book/EBook editions, remember though that you will be required to purchase/generate an updated ISBN/Barcode number Throughout history, many authors have often renamed their original book titles at a later time, often increasing book sales on a monumental scale.

Original Book Title:	**Revised Book Title:**
First Impressions	Pride and Prejudice
All's Well That Ends Well	Gone with the Wind
The Last Man in Europe	1984
Second Coming	Salem's Lot
The High-Bouncing Lover	The Great Gatsby
Strangers from Within	Lord of the Flies
Men Who Hate Women	The Girl with the Dragon Tattoo
The Un-Dead	Dracula
Atticus	To Kill a Mockingbird

Catch a glimpse of your title and place yourself in the potential reader's shoes questioning: Who? (Main character), Where? (Location), How? (Storyline), When? (Timeframe), Why? (book theme/plot). What does the title envision and does it entice the reader into wanting more, prompting a click on the "buy now" tab? Such a decision takes the reader mere seconds, so make your book the one they choose.

Although it may appear straightforward, choosing a book title is one of the more difficult aspects of writing a book. Some authors may already have a title in mind

Part One: Book Completion

before their opening lines, halfway through or not until completion of the first draft. Be patient and take your time during this thought-provoking process. Browsing book titles often help to narrow down those final choices including tips like these:

- Brainstorm for ideas using catchy keywords/phrases
- Jot down multiple titles and use a process of elimination
- Use main book theme in title
- Get feedback from trusted readers/friends
- Intrigue the reader's attention into wanting to know more
- Include your main character in title
- Use a minimum of five words or less up to a maximum of 10/12
- Relax and follow your intuition/certainty with the final choice

*According to literary guidelines, the use of pronouns, verbs, adjectives and adverbs are usually capitalized in book titles, songs and articles. First and last words always use capital letters while "a/an" and "the" are not. This also applies to the use of any subtitle.

Choosing a title for a fiction or non-fiction book will differ greatly, so let's separate them out and gather some ideas on choices in the process:

Fiction Books/Titles are created from the writer's imagination to lure in prospective readers without obstacles getting in the way. A fiction title should resonate with just a few words. Envision most fiction as seeking an escape from everyday living and your title should help fill that need. Summarizing your storyline into a few words will not only describe the theme but also help to draw the reader in. This undertaking will require both in-depth analysis as well as pure creativity. A great fictional title should always intrigue the potential reader without giving away too much of the plot. Last but not least, the secret of a good title invites the reader to want to start reading the book immediately.

Non-Fiction Books/Titles often include subtitles and usually refer to a literature based on fact. Subjects can include a variety of topics like self-help, autobiographies/biographies, documentaries, history and narrated events. The chosen title should directly address what the reader will gain from reading this book. Creating an individual need will only add to your book's attraction.

Consider your final book title choice as captivating combined with book cover design. A perfect title is one that also fits along the spine.

Guess what the top ten most popular book titles of all time are?

1. Don Quixote – Miguel De Cervantes
2. Lord of the Rings – R.R. Tolkien
3. Harry Potter and the Sorcerer's Stone – J.K. Rowling
4. And Then There Were None – Agatha Christie
5. Alice's Adventures in Wonderland – Lewis Carroll
6. The Lion, the Witch and the Wardrobe – C.S. Lewis
7. Pinocchio – Carlo Collodi
8. The Catcher in the Rye – J.D. Salinger
9. Anne of Green Gables – L.M. Montgomery
10. 20.000 Leagues Under the Sea – Jules Verne

Now might be the perfect time to give your book that final once over before heading into the exciting world of cover design paired with color palette, book genre, etc. On a final note, remember it's okay to fail or fall, as long as it's always forwards and not backwards. You are now well on your way to becoming a self-published author, so let's head to the next important stage, shall we?

"Let yourself go. You're bound to bloom."
- Unknown

Part Two: Getting Published
Chapter 1: You Can Judge a book by its cover

"A year from now, you may wish you had started today."
—Karen Lamb

At very first glance, a book cover design (followed by title) plays an integral role in garnering an online click or getting passed over. The entire process takes mere seconds, making book cover design so crucially important. Why not have yours stand out among all the other competitive books out there? Your cover could end up mesmerizing the viewer towards the next captivating read on their nightstand or device.

As addressed in the previous chapter, the innovative creation of an original, yet catchy title takes you on an exciting yet winding path. The very same applies here with the combination of title and cover. Remember, you only get that one first impression, so here's the chance to make it "Unforgettable." Stay true to all those original/creative ideas that captured your inspiration as it will resonate in your finalized choice of book cover.

Aside from the title, creating a book cover design will mark the results of all your devoted energies. Enjoy the experience as this is where your artistic talents will really get to shine. Unless artfully inclined, working alongside a talented artistic/graphic designer can also add a magical essence as your dream/vision slowly becomes a reality. You may want to do research in your local area for a talented graphic designer, fitting in with your ideas and budget. Some writers even create a personal Dream/Mood board to both inspire and help with an upcoming book cover design.

The common phrase of "Don't judge a book by its cover" becomes a blatant reality in the book industry with potential readers making a split-second decision on whether to buy your book. Once again, take your time during this painstaking design process as it introduces your book to the world.

As you embark on the many twists and turns towards final cover design, sit back and enjoy this once in a lifetime ride. Along with choosing a title and making your mind up on the perfect cover, the rest will feel like a piece of cake.

A successful book cover will always create a mood for the viewer, tempting them further towards wanting to read the inside. When professionally done, the cover also reflects a much higher book quality. In contrast, a cheaper or homemade book design creates the opposite effect; lower sales. Allow your striking cover design to introduce the theme and tone of your book. If correctly paired with the subject genre, you are setting yourself on the right course. Your final cover design could mean the difference between a hit and a flop. Take precious time to carefully craft your best work as this book cover will soon become your billboard towards future readership.

Tips on creating a memorable book cover:
1. Make it easy to read/compelling at first sight
2. Choose the correct font/background
3. Space the title with use of a focal point to stand out
4. Contrasting colors blend better/easier on the eye
5. Use a teaser from the book to attract attention
6. Seek the assistance of professional design
7. Use visual elements from your book/storyline
8. Keep it simple
9. Explore your imagination
10. Test multiple cover options

Before you begin, take a long browse through books in your chosen genre at home, online, in libraries,

Part Two: Getting Published   33

bookstores and beyond. This may afford you some innovative ideas on which design direction to take. You might ask yourself the following based on the cover:
- Has the author taken time on a professional cover or does it resemble the result of a hasty decision?
- Does the cover reflect the overall book theme?
- Is the title/cover engaging enough to catch the reader's attention?
- Is the cover clear and easy to read even via a thumbnail image?
- Does the audience want to know more?
- Is it memorable and original?
- Does it entice me to click/buy?
(split-second decision)

    I will bet the covers that stood out to you the most were carefully designed to captivate the viewer. Once you have worked this out, the complexity of selecting a dazzling cover will become much clearer. By now, you have realized the impact your book cover generates towards the reader's decision on whether to click/purchase your book.

    If this is the first of an upcoming book series, perhaps you might want to incorporate an initial design that can be linked to future titles in order to build your brand.

    The front cover font should always remain consistent with the back cover. Experiment with multiple fonts and sizes until reaching a comfort level that fits in line with your title. The creation of a central focal point with color contrast will always stand out more on a book display/screen. Did you know what you finally decide upon will capture the overall mood of your book title/genre? Check out some of the following color choices and suggested interpretations that could make or break the book/overview of your cover:

Dark red: - Passion, dominance, prestige
Orange: - Positive, confident, dynamic
Pale yellow: - Warm, friendly, approachable
Bold yellow: - Ambition, motivation, creative
Dark blue: - Truth, sincerity, intuition
Purple: - Mystery, fantasy, spirituality
Grey: - Prestige, wisdom, sophistication
Pink: - Playful, youth, innocence
White: - Clean, simple, self-confident
Black: - Power, suspense, authority
Brown: - Nature, organic, comfortable

A creative blend of these colors adds impact on the cover design with the following combinations: (www.tailorbrands.com)

Blue/green/yellow   - Wisdom and youth
Red/yellow/blue   - Artistic and fun
Beige/blue/green   - Confidence and creative
Peach/maroon   - Peaceful and elegant
Black/orange   - Thrill and mystery
Royal blue/yellow   - Optimism and trust

You can see how your cover color choices most definitely create a mood for the viewer on whether to open/click or dismiss your presentation. Allow your final palette to pop as well as attracting the reader/viewer at the same time. That may seem harder than it sounds, but practice really does make perfect. Online, you can discover a host of programs like Shutterstock, Photoshop, AdobeInDesign, Lulu and many more. In the end, be in no doubt you will make your own choices towards the creation of a formidable cover.

While the front cover is the first image seen, the back cover carries equal importance (although not required for Ebooks/Kindle versions) in displaying informative book details. There should always remain a conceptual continuance of the front cover image with the same color contrast on all sides. A compact and detailed book summary should be consistent with any selected book blurbs. A **Blurb**

Part Two: Getting Published 35

can include a quote from a valued reader who has enjoyed your book with a brief comment. It can also consist of a short and catchy summary that best describes the book.

Remember a while back when you sent those writing samples to avid readers among family and friends? You could now request them to compose a phrase describing their reaction. Use a few of these blurbs on the back cover or in your book introduction, if you like. In addition, the creation of a book blurb provides an additional tool during the promotional stages.

Make sure to leave an empty space on the bottom right corner of the back book cover for placement of your ISBN and barcode numbers. If desired, you can also add a small author photo along the bottom left side. Last but not least, the spine of your book will need to be designed. The spine measurement will relate to your book's thickness, depending on the number of pages of text. Once again, the colors should match on both the front and back cover and displays the title and author with perhaps a small image. Remember this useful tip: **You can always Judge and Sell a book by its cover!**

Did you know that most best-selling books that went on to become number one movies all shared something in common? What was that? A captivating book cover that shouted out…READ ME! BUY ME! The following are rated among the top box office hits:

Jaws, To Kill a Mockingbird, 1984, The Wizard of Oz, Jurassic Park, Psycho, The Godfather, The Great Gatsby, The Shining, Les Miserables, The Hobbit, Harry Potter, Twilight, Into The Storm, Oceans 11, The Tale of Peter Rabbit, etc.

Let this serve as an Inspirational reminder that you too can come up with a Magical book cover all of your own creation. Who knows where it may all lead?

"When you have a dream, you've got to grab it and never let it go."

–Carol Burnett

Part Two: Getting Published
Chapter 2: Setting up ISBNs and Barcodes

"You are never too old to set a new goal or dream a new dream."

—C.S. Lewis

In order to self-publish your book, you will usually be required to purchase an ISBN/ International Standard Book Identification number along with a barcode for each separate title/version. Take for example; should you decide to release both a paperback and kindle, two ISBNs will be necessary. FYI: Although Amazon etc. do not require an ISBN number/ barcode for the EBook version, you will still need to register the numbers with Bowkers/Myidentfiers.com.

    This ISBN number will forever serve as both the identifier of your book title, subtitle, author, format, book description, selected language, publication date and year of copyright. The assigned thirteen digit number and five digit barcode (purchased separately) will appear along the bottom right corner on your book's back cover. This EAN barcode/ International Article Number will list the book price whenever scanned at a store register as well as in global trade. As a reminder; each book format or selected publisher, will require separate ISBNs and barcodes, which makes it a good idea to buy packages of multiple numbers. The current price for one ISBN number is $129 while a package of ten will only set you back $295 (a 76% discount). A single barcode costs $25, with a pack of six at $138. (2021 prices)

    Before we continue, it is important to note that if you wrote your book with the sole intention of printing only for local distribution to family/friends etc. the allocation of an ISBN will not be deemed necessary. However, if you decide not to purchase an ISBN number, you may be affected by the

Part Two: Getting Published 37

following circumstances:
- Your book will not be listed in **Books in Print**, a vast bibliographic database of book titles that aids in both the search/discovery of books
- Some online retailers may refuse to stock your book
- Your book may not be available to the section of your audience who prefer reading physical books

(www.editage.com) Bowker remains the world's leading provider of ISBN numbers and barcodes for published books that include the USA, UK and Australia. * For book releases in the UK etc., please visit www.nielsentitleeditor.com and for AU/NZ visit www.myidentifiers.com.au In today's literary world, Bowker is the most trusted source of bibliographic information designed for book discovery and acquisition for libraries worldwide.

In the USA, you will find all required ISBN details at www.bowker.com or www.myidentifiers.com If an online publisher offers you a free ISBN number, I would highly recommend instead purchasing your own as it will always recognize you as the sole owner/publisher of your written work As an example, Amazon KDP might offer a free ISBN for your book's Kindle version but that same book cannot be distributed/sold on any other online site. (You will need to have a separate PDF, Mobi or EPUB book file) Owning your own ISBN number however will allow you to market you book anywhere in the world.

When perusing the aforementioned websites, take plenty of time to scroll through each detailed online section as it will walk you through the entire process. Before you begin though, ensure you have access to all of your downloadable files, such as book cover, book file, genre, publisher, relevant keywords, website, brief book summary, author bio etc. The more detailed information (metadata) provided, the larger impact you will make on those future book buyers. At any time, feel free to log in to your account to add/edit data; after all, you are the book owner. If you later decide to update your first book with additional pages and/or corrections, it will incorporate creating a second edition. It will therefore require a new/separate ISBN and EAN barcode. In addition, if your book is translated into another language, the same protocol applies.

Useful tips before logging on to www.myidentifiers.com
     Once you have set up an account and purchased one/package of ten ISBN numbers, your book details are ready to be entered. Each individual number will be assigned to your individual book versions (EBook, paperback or hardback). The rest (if you purchased a package) remain unassigned until you update editions, release a new book etc. and will never expire. All numbers identify you as the sole owner/publisher/author. There are four primary sections where your information is uploaded:

1. Title & Cover: Title/subtitle, book cover (JPEG only), book description (up to 350 words), author bio, date of publication/copyright, language, Library of Congress control number (if applicable)
2. Contributors: Authors & contributors and main genre
3. Format & Size: EBook, paperback or hardback format, sizing dimensions & weight, number of pages/illustrations, subject genres (choose two)
4. Sales & Pricing: Publisher (you, if self-published), publication date, title status (on demand), target audience & age range, pricing, currency, country of sales distribution (all minor details here not necessary during initial set up)

    *Once the final book prices for Amazon etc. are finalized, your ISBN/barcode will show the price along the top right. When you have your book/s registered with Bowkers/Myidentifiers, go to your book dashboard and click on the book which you want to download your ISBN/barcode label. To the right, you will see your assigned ISBN you have already chosen. On the right again, you will now generate the EAN/barcode. You will see two variations to download; PDF and EPS. In order for your book to be scanned at bookstore registers etc. you will need to choose the EPS/Vector one as

Part Two: Getting Published   39

it can be enlarged without any changes to the barcodes. You may now share, download and/or print your book label. As a reminder, you have to scroll down to the very bottom of the page where your label will be on the left side.

To encourage you along this part of the journey, the chairman of Bowker International ISBN Agency recently announced: "The self-publishing business seems poised to continue to post solid gains. As more authors take advantage of the abundant tools now available to publish, distribute and market their own book, we expect self-publishing to continue to grow at a steady pace."

*Should an ISBN number be obtained from any other source (Amazon, Kobo etc.) it may not identify the name of the publisher correctly and thereby hinder future business in the book industry supply chain. Note: It's always best to buy your own.

Would you believe the trend of becoming a self-published author has only been in existence for the past decade so…..how TRENDY are you going to be?

Some additional details on the importance of owning an ISBN:
- Ensures location of your book worldwide
- Links to essential book information
- Enables efficient marketing and distribution
- Stored in global book and print database regularly consulted by publishers, libraries and retailers worldwide

On a final note, your ISBN numbers and barcodes will never expire. So what are you waiting for?

"It is our attitude at the beginning of a difficult task which more than anything else, will affect its successful outcome."

–William James

Part Two: Getting Published
Chapter Three: Book Format, Genre & Metadata

"The secret of getting ahead is getting started."
—Mark Twain

All books are mainly classified into two categories: fiction and non-fiction, with multiple genres/sub genres encompassed in between. The accurate placement of book correctly matched with genre will incorporate the following features:
- Makes it more profitable for the author
- Meets reader expectations
- Organizes book information to make for an easier read
- Helps establish a core readership
- Used as a classification tool to provide specific literature type

    The book genre that best describes your written masterpiece not only introduces you to the world as an author, but also helps target potential future followers towards a preferred reading niche. Throughout the process of choosing your genre, imagine the location/category of the book store/library where you would most like your book to be placed.
    "What comes first, the genre or the concept? The first step to choosing between the screenplay genres is to find the one that best serves your idea. Most scripts fail because the writer didn't choose the best genre to tell their story. Each genre will take a story idea in radically different directions." (utoledo.edu)
Help with choosing a Genre for your book:
- Always write what you love and choose genre later
- Experiment with a few different genres

Part Two: Getting Published 41

- Think about your reader's expectations
- Align your story with the correct genre
- Observe pros and cons of possible genres
- Pick primary genre/s most marketable

According to www.kirkus.com, the most popular publishing trends for 2021 are the following:

- Escapist fiction
- Better quality and quantity
- Greater diversity
- Artificial intelligence
- Virtual books

However, with relation to bulk book sales, Romance still remains the number one genre across the world today. This is closely followed by Mystery, Science Fiction, Thriller, Young Adult, Children's Fiction, Self-Help/Inspiration and Biography/Autobiography. Browse through the top selling categories on Amazon by book listings, sales, algorithms, ratings and reviews. If you happen to be a writer of Romance/Fiction, you might introduce your first book in a series as readers love to follow along with their favorite characters. A prime example of the hugely popular romance book series would be "Outlander" by Diana Gabaldon. Her books/series incorporate multiple genres including romance, historical fiction, mystery, adventure and science fiction fantasy. If writing a popular book genre is significant to you, it would be worthwhile to conduct additional research to assist with your overall writing style. This also helps create a larger impact on book presentation towards targeting potential new readers/sales.

Most publishing platforms generally allow books to include two or three genres at the most, making it imperative to choose wisely. On a positive note, you may also select additional sub-category options throughout the uploading and metadata process. On Amazon for example, via your author page, there is ample opportunity to expand your book genres.

Metadata refers to a set of data that describes and gives information about other data that is used to classify, organize and be placed in the correct location. In this instance, metadata is used throughout the reading world to direct libraries and booksellers on where best to place your book. It includes the title, subtitle, author, genre, format, page count, book size etc. You will soon become familiar with this term as you begin publishing your work on multiple platforms like Ingram Spark, Draft2Digital, Kobo and many more. By providing metadata, you are bringing your book to life by displaying all the important details of your work. Take full advantage of this opportunity to showcase the hidden elements of your book within the metadata to impress future clients.

It may also prove useful to create a metadata PDF document that will save precious time whenever communicating with prospective vendors. The use of ten main keywords or less will also fine-tune the essential details of your book. Remember the more metadata included, the more you will draw in readers/booksellers. For example, if your book is about travels in Ireland, you could add specific fun facts like; how to serve the perfect pint of Guinness or kissing the Blarney Stone etc. Original metadata will not only attract new readers but also make your book pop.

A typical Metadata sheet should include the following book details:
- Book title, subtitle, author, genre, subgenres and keywords
- Book description, brief summary
- Author biography
- Publication date, edition, formats, page count, trim size, price
- ISBN numbers, BISAC codes
- Author website, blog and/or social media details

*If you find the word **Metadata** overwhelming; don't worry

Part Two: Getting Published

as you have basically already added all of this detailed information while submitting your book details online.

A **BISAC code** (Book Industry Standards and Communication) basically informs retailers where your book should be shelved. It is used by worldwide book suppliers to further categorize books based on topical content. Bisac codes included with metadata will help to further broaden the reach and depth of your book. Select the most relevant keyword/s that accurately describes your book/content as they will guide the reader/buyer towards a possible purchase. In addition, Bisac codes are used to narrow down a book's subject, genre and reading level.

Check out www.bisg.org for a thorough FAQ on BISAC Subject Codes and where/how to use them in your book description etc.

Remember the last time you browsed for a new book at the library/bookshop, and you picked one up to check it out? Did the cover, title, back cover, blurb pique your interest? (or not). You may have simply replaced it back on the shelf, depending on the overall book presentation.

By now, you have discovered how essential the initial look of your book title/cover translates into attracting new readers. The summary and metadata also adds to the icing on the cake towards that future read.

Quality metadata can either indicate future book sales or not. It reflects upon whether details have been submitted in a professional format. Have fun using your choice of keywords that make your book stand out versus the same old boring and typical descriptions. This is your baby after all, so enjoy the ride.

"Do not go where the path may lead, go instead where there is no path and leave a trail."
–Ralph Waldo Emerson

Part One: Book Completion
Chapter Four: Time to upload those book files

"Nothing is IMPOSSIBLE; the word itself is I'M POSSIBLE!"

–Audrey Hepburn

Have you reached your final word/page count at this stage? It's no surprise that over the past decade; thanks to a social media uptick and screen time, there has been a decline in the average reader's attention span. Newly-released books have decreased in length by over 40% (from an average of 465 to 270) making every single word you write count. 50% of the top bestsellers usually range anywhere from 250 to 350 total pages.

Should you use single or double-spaced lines? Publishing industry standards typically require double-spaced lines and if unsure, here's how to create it:
- On Microsoft Word, Press Ctrl-A (Windows) to choose text
- Then select Format > Paragraph > Spacing - select double-space option
- On MAC, Command-A
- On Google Docs, select all text again and navigate to Format > Line spacing
- Using a writing program like Scrivener, the formatting will likely be done already when you go to export your manuscript; double check though (www.writersedit.com)

As with the cover and title, the interior and layout of a book are equally important. Use of appropriate font, an organized layout and reading flow will all help to create both a memorable and enjoyable read.

If you happen to be computer savvy and familiar with techie terminologies, then go ahead with book

Part Two: Getting Published

formatting requirements. If not, it would be wise to seek the assistance of an IT expert. Believe me; your book will exude a much more professional, polished finish as it becomes a permanent fixture in the literary world.

Every published book consists of front, body and back matter:

<u>Front Matter</u>: - Title page, Copyright page, Acknowledgment/Dedication page, Table of Contents
<u>Body</u>: - Foreword/Introduction, Chapters, Epilogue/Afterword
<u>Back Matter</u>: - Acknowledgments, Photos, Recipes, Bibliography/Glossary, Appendix, Endnotes (review requests), About the Author

Book formatting translates into how your manuscript looks/reads as a final product. It is helpful to include an inviting layout for your future reader consisting of a script that is neither too big nor too small. Lines should normally be double-spaced without extra spaces between paragraphs to display a uniform and neat presentation. This also includes single spaces after each period. Attention to detail will be key in this painstaking process, so take all the time you need. For a final proof reading along with researching similar books within your genre, the following **formatting tips** may prove helpful:

- Establish your overall format with fonts, tabs, margins *(more below)
- Table of Contents includes all front, main and back matter including chapter headings, page numbers and bibliography/glossary
- Copyright page indicates copyright notice/year, ISBN number/s, Library of Congress control number, credits to editors, photographers, illustrators, original country of print
- Dedication page, Introduction, chapter titles and subtitles etc.
- Page numbers, headers & footers
- Line-spacing, indenting and paragraph breaks

- Illustrations or photos
- Bio summary and/or website
- Book or Amazon review request

* As a reminder, book photos and images always help tell a more compelling story but try to keep them to a minimum as the printing costs will only rise. The most important image should appear on your book cover which by itself can tell a thousand words.

Fonts, Tabs & Margins:

Although Times New Roman/12 point remains the most popular publishing industry standard, Arial, Bembo, Courier, Janson, Palatino etc. are also commonly used. (FYI; Verdana/12 point is used throughout this book) Serif fonts (decorative stroke at the end of each letter) are easier on the reader's eye than sans-serif (without) especially with so much reading nowadays on bright screens. Georgia and Helvetica tend to work best for a kindle read while Baskerville, Garamond and Minion are among Google favorites. A regular font size of between 10 and 12 is normally recommended.

The U.S. standard page size is 8.5 x 11 inches, using one-inch margins on all sides, top, bottom, right and left. This maintains a uniform appearance along with a half-inch indentation for each new paragraph (simply using tab will work).

The **Sizing & Trim** will affect the final page count. The larger your book size, the lower the page count, while the smaller size reflects a higher page count. Once again, following the research of your genre, you decide what works best for your individual needs. Here are some general sizings examples for you to consider that are commonly used in the publishing world:

- 4.5" x 6.87, 5" x 8, 5.25 x 8, 6 x 9 FICTION
- 7.5 x 7.5, 7 x 10, 8 x 10, 10 x 10 CHILDREN'S
- 6 x 9, 7 x 10, 8.5 x 11 TEXTBOOKS
- 5.5 x 8.5, 6 x 9, 7 x 10 NON-FICTION
- 5.25 X 8, 5.5 X 8.5 MEMOIR

Part Two: Getting Published

- 8.5 X 8.5, 11 X 14, 12 X 12 ART, PHOTOGRAPHY, COOKBOOKS, TRAVEL, COFFEE TABLE BOOK

    An important aspect of formatting may include minor last-minute editing especially if you end up with an almost blank page with just one sentence. (*Publishers detest blank book pages)
    You may need to make final minor adjustments in order to give your book that overall tailored appearance. If you have written your book using Microsoft Word or PDF format, the uploading process should prove a relatively smooth one. However if you used a different format, it might be wise to transfer the files over as most publishers will accept both uploading formats.
    Each individual publisher may request a variety of book-format specifications based on page sizes, margins, fonts, number of pages, front and back cover images, attached inside images etc. The more formatted your book files meet the publisher's requirements, the less stressful your experience. Be patient and kind to yourself during this crucial and painstaking process. You are close to crossing the final stretch of your book presentation as both a polished and professional masterpiece.
    Check out <u>Kindle Previewer</u> especially if you are creating an EBook/Kindle version on Amazon. This is a free desktop application that allows you to view how your book will appear upon delivery to kindle customers. You will also have the chance to detect those last-minute adjustments. Scrolling through your entire book, you may also catch any unforeseen errors before final publishing. Before you feel ready for that final upload on the online platform of your choice, there are tutorials that can help before beginning the process. This way, you will avoid overlooking any minor hiccups as you go. On some publishing sites such as <u>Ingramspark and Amazon</u>, you can order a test book copy to ensure the cover (matte/gloss), insides, print, page count etc. are all correct and

to your liking. Any last changes/corrections can be made at this point before going live to 90% of bookstores/libraries around the world.

Once you have uploaded all required book files, most sites have a turnaround time of up to seventy-two hours. Once complete, you will be notified that your book has been revised and is now eligible to be published on the selected site. You will have one last option to preview your file but bear in mind, once you hit the OK tab, you are officially published with your book now live on the internet. At this point, you can now order your very own official copy. Although you may pay a little more, it is much faster to order as a regular customer (Amazon only). Congratulations, you are now a published author!

"What you get by achieving your goals is not as important as what you become by achieving your goals."

- Zig Ziglar

Part Two: Getting Published
Chapter 5: Where to Publish?

"Believe you can and you're halfway there."
–Theodore Roosevelt

Inching closer to becoming a published author, you just might reach a dilemma on exactly where to get published. So many choices can be confusing while frustrating at the same time. Allow me to run through some of the multiple options available to help ease your weary mind. Always remember, since you own the rights to your book/s (via ISBN number etc.) you can choose to publish/remove your edition anywhere at any time.

*In the traditional publishing world, authors have additional pressures on marketing/selling their book while earning @ 7.5% per copy, with little to no say on book price. If they happen to have an agent, there goes a further loss of 15% on sales income. Finally, all book tour expenses of hotels, meals and transport etc. will generally be deducted from book sales to boot. Not such a great deal, unless you happen to be a celebrity or well-known writer.

Firstly, there are many self-published authors who have chosen to write, edit and **print their own books** (via a local commercial printer), selling them directly to the public. At any given time, they may have a hundred or more copies on hand stored in their home/garage. Here are some pros and cons to this method:

PROS: Works well for established local/national individuals/authors with acclaimed books, series, self-help guides, local community/countrywide connections, popular websites, high social media activity, academic and literary networks, socially active events etc., always available on hand for in-person sales, complete control of sales output, no ISBN/barcodes are necessary

CONS: Costly to order books in bulk, takes up storage space, responsible for packaging/shipping/returns, heavy to transport/set up at events, limited online audience, limited inventory, limited online capacity of look inside book option, etc.

Obviously, the author will garner a full 100% royalty in book sales, providing he/she has a potential and established readership base. Some authors have chosen this route to maintain a level of privacy away from conglomerate giants like Amazon etc. It will all be your own individual choice…You can also do both.

On a global level, the printing level of self-published books will reach sales of @ $821 billion by 2022, mostly driven by digital and POD (Print On Demand).

Okay now, with **AMAZON** the elephant in the literary room, let's check out what all the fuss is about, shall we? In July 1994, Jeff Bezos founded Amazon naming it after the largest river in the world. In the first three years, only books were sold competing with reputable booksellers like Barnes & Noble, etc. Bezos believed books had an infinite selection capacity due to their extensive and never ending categories.

Today, Amazon has become the world's largest online book retailer generating @ 50% of the printed market and @ 80% of ebooks. 40% of all top-selling eBooks on Amazon originate from self-published authors like you. This could be the golden opportunity for you and your book to make that unique impact. At any given time, there are over five billion people online around the world. Any one of those individuals could be searching for a new book to read/feel inspired by/change careers/self-help etc.

Keep in mind the most successful self-published authors on Amazon already own a series of books that have taken years to build on their platform. Fiction books

Part Two: Getting Published

still remain among the top-sellers. Amazon Marketing can also prove worthwhile with additional clicks/reviews to boost interest towards your latest book release (older book).

www.kdp.amazon.com

* "KDP allows you to self-publish ebooks and paperbacks for free. We give you direct access to your book on Amazon and allow you to create a product detail page for your book. It also gives you the option to expand your book's availability on a global scale, making it more accessible for readers around the world."

Basic steps to setting up an author account with Amazon/KDP:

- Set up account with user ID and PW
- Enter all book details/metadata etc.
- Verify book publishing rights, ISBN# etc.
- Select Royalties (paperback 60%/eBook 35% or 70% etc.)
- Target future Amazon readers/customers with book genre/category
- Select a book release date
- Upload book file/s
- Preview/review emailed book copy via Kindle Previewer
- Order an author copy before final book release
- OK final file and book is automatically LIVE (unless selected release date)

You decide which royalty amounts suit you the best but remember the printing costs will be deducted from the royalties. Take for example, a paperback book sold @ $11.95 with a 60% royalty. After printing, the author will receive a final payment of @ $4.07 @ 60 days following the month of the book sale.

*From time to time, you may see your Amazon book price reduced in order to promote book sales but fear not; you will still receive a full royalty payment on any sale during this promotional period.

Once your book/s are established online with Amazon, here is some helpful advice to help navigate the site and further enhance your book sales potential.

Along the top of the page, you will see four main criteria headers:
1. Bookshelf: This is where you create all of your book content, details, pricing, edit/changes, order author copies, book editions on view
2. Reports: All your book sales/formats are available via date, preorders, promotions, generated sales reports etc.
3. Community: Gives you the chance to connect with fellow authors, create advertising with Amazon etc.
4. Marketing: KDP Select and other programs available

Once your eBook (this service only applies to electronic books) has been set up on the Amazon website, you are eligible to join KDP Select which enables the following:

For a 90-day period, you can promote your book by offering a discounted price for 7 days and/or free for 5 days as part of a Countdown Deal. You can start at a lower price and gradually increase the price by the seventh day of promotion. AMAZON has a specific following of KDP Select readers/whale readers who constantly search for new book discounts. Even if your ebook is discounted down to 99 cents, you will still be paid a full 70% royalty. This is a great way to get your ebook out there, although I recommend ending this program after the 90 day period as your ebook can only be published/available on Amazon. Also, make sure to disable "expanded distribution", especially if publishing on other sites. Otherwise, this prevents future earnings from sites such as IngramSpark, Smashwords, Draft2Digital,

Part Two: Getting Published 53

Barnes & Noble/Nook, apple/iTunes etc.

If you ever violate Amazon's terms, your book can be deleted/banned. It is wise to do extensive research on whether to use this service for the first three months (or not) to help with additional publicity for your eBook. Delve into what will work best for you and your book release.

Throughout your KDP Select enrolment (not necessary/your choice) don't forget to explore other avenues to promote your eBook such as via Kindle Unlimited and Kindle Owners Lending Library where you are paid according to the number of book pages read.

*Once the three-month period is over, remember to cancel your KDP Select membership and you are now free to publish anywhere online that you like.

*Should you decide to publish on additional online platforms, remember to cancel your book's Unlimited Distribution with Amazon before heading to those sites. If all of this sounds confusing, leave out Unlimited Distribution altogether when setting up your book on Amazon. Make sense?

www.ingramspark.com
INGRAMSPARK is another publishing option for all formats of your new book. "Established nearly 50 years ago, Ingram Book Group (IBG) is the largest book distributor in the world, serving 40,000+ book retailers worldwide, of both the brick and mortar and online variety. So, in a sense, it is a very big deal for authors and publishers to be locked into publishing with IngramSpark." www.selfpublishing.com

The **Global Connect** option with INGRAMSPARK allows your book to be Printed On Demand (POD) at their many facilities in UK, France, Italy, Spain, Germany, Poland, Russia, Australia, South Korea, China, Brazil and India. Additional countries are being added on a constant basis. Local channels in these countries can order/receive printed orders at a much faster rate.

Basic steps to setting up an account with IngramSpark:
- Set up an account with user ID and PW
- Pay $49 fee for paperback or hardback
- Pay $25 fee for ebook (free if added to paperback/hardback)
- Enter all book details/metadata etc.
- Verify book publishing rights, ISBN# etc. (you must have your own ISBN#)
- Select retailers book discount (53-55% norm) and returnable options
- (You can choose your own discount, starting from 30%)
- Order book copy/proof before final publish

For some added perspective on both Amazon and Ingramspark (feel free to use both platforms) here is a list of pros and cons for your perusal.

PROS and CONS of publishing with AMAZON:
PROS:
- FREE to publish paperback/eBook or hardback (new option)
- 200 million Prime members worldwide
- 197+ million monthly Amazon visitors
- FREE book edits/revision (new ISBN# required)
- Faster delivery with Amazon Prime
- Ongoing/new book marketing series/programs
- Higher author royalty payment
- Ability to connect with readers/authors via blogs etc.

CONS:
- Books generally unavailable in brick and mortar stores
- Royalty payments have printing costs deducted first
- Book quality is slightly inferior to the one from IngramSpark
- Marketing campaign is costly

PROS and CONS of publishing with INGRAMSPARK:

Part Two: Getting Published

PROS:
- Book available on AMAZON, Barnes & Noble, Apple iTunes & Worldwide via Global Connect
- Book available to libraries/bookstores around the world
- Book format/costs/how it works options before publishing
- Author discounts @ book fairs, promotional publishing sites etc.
- Book quality is slightly superior to the one from Amazon
- Hardback book choices in blue/grey cloth excellent quality
- Free online publishing/promotional courses/podcasts etc.
- Monthly educational newsletters to enhance publishing/sales

CONS:
- $49 and $25 publishing costs and revisions
- Returns accepted, i.e. paid by author (expensive if bookstore orders)
- 20 copies and only 5 are sold – author can either purchase the returned books with extra shipping costs/have them destroyed
- Lower book royalty
- Slower book delivery time

In July 2021, Amazon launched a brand new serialized platform for fiction writers called KINDLE VELLA where authors can publish stories on a weekly basis. The episodes range from 600 to 5000 words. The first three story episodes are free. After which, additional episodes are purchased on the app using reader tokens. The author earns a 50% revenue along with a launch bonus based upon customer activity/engagement. Prizes are awarded for Stories of the Week and featured by Amazon. This makes a wonderful outlet for authors/

readers to engage/receive ongoing feedback.

One token equates to 100 words. Token prices start @ $1.99 for 200 tokens, increasing to $14.99 for 1700.

*For more details check out the Amazon website or the IOS Kindle app.

Check out www.loc.gov if you would like your newly-released book to be added to the **Library of Congress** in Washington D.C. You will need to set up an account, complete an Application To Participate, while obtaining an account, ID and password. It can prove a timely process, so follow the guidelines carefully. There is no cost to apply. Most importantly, two physical book copies will need to be submitted/sent within three months of publication.

***The following (mostly) fiction websites/apps are free to the author.**

RADISH (2016) is a mobile reading app for serialized bingeable **fiction** writers supported via a micropayment platform. Readers are encouraged to test book content by reading early chapters/episodes for free or via inexpensive micro payments (@20-30 cents) prior to a book launch/release. Series are produced TV-style with episodes created in house and writers hired per project. A typical story might comprise of ten chapters with min 1500 words, including a detailed outline. Daily/weekly serialized stories will attract new readers and showcase authors as part of an additional revenue outlet. www.radishfiction.com

WATTPAD is an upgraded version for **fan fiction** readers and invites new/established authors to write in specific genres. Authors can communicate with readers via email in relation to new chapters/series etc. Reader votes are cast on chapters, storylines etc. allowing writers the opportunity to edit, re-adjust storyline, characters based on feedback. 90 million users interact on a regular basis on this site with the slogan: "WHERE STORIES LIVE!" www.wattpad.com

Part Two: Getting Published

INKITT is yet another digital-publishing platform based in Berlin, Germany for fiction writers. An additional reader-based site where a computer algorithm predicts book success based on reader behavior. For published stories, authors can receive quarterly payments but unlike Wattpad, readers' votes are not available to be viewed by the author.   www.inkitt.com

DREAME is a private equity firm in Singapore who created a popular fiction ready app for writers/readers to share content. It is primarily targeted for a female audience. Top ranking submitted stories can potentially earn decent monthly royalties via a pay to read program. Writers will need to upload their story/book and apply for a contract that will either be accepted/rejected.
www.Dreame.com

COMMAFUL is designed for short story writers and poets who like to add illustrations which enable their stories to come to life. There is a strong fan engagement between reader/writer with helpful feedback in support of new/established authors.   www.commaful.com

MEDIUM is an online platform where creative writers upload content and connect with regular readers by stories sent directly to their inboxes. You can earn a regular income by joining the Medium Partner Program. Anyone on the internet can read your stories on Medium which has a huge library audience. Thoughts/ideas are shared on multiple subjects.   www.medium.com

   *Among additional and reputable online publishing platforms to choose from are **Draft2Digital** who will add your eBook to huge retailers like OVERDRIVE (libraries worldwide), Baker & Taylor, PublishDrive, BorrowBox (UK/ AU libraries), Bibliotheca, Tolino, Scribd, Vivlio etc. **Smashwords** is another eBook library distributor etc. Most of these free online sites typically take a 10% sales commission with the author earning @ 40% in royalty payments based on the eBook listing price. You can set up your minimum income level before getting paid. For example, once you reach fifty dollars in sales income, you can expect payment.

On online websites like the aforementioned, you can also factor in the best pricing option based on comparable books in your genre.

When all is said and done, it is vital to do your own extensive research on any potential online publishing platform before diving into to any new venture. The bigger the book platform you create, the more potential exciting new readers will discover your writing. * All the patient time and effort put forth will in time eventually reap rewards in multiple ways...have patience.

"Never limit yourself because of others' limited imagination; never limit others because of your own limited imagination."

–Mae Jemisom

Part Three:
Let The Promotions Begin
Chapter One: How/Where to start?

*"Go confidently in the direction of your dreams.
Live the life you have imagined"*
                                        -Henry David Thoreau

According to Bookscan, 93% of all new self-published books will sell no more than one hundred copies with an average earnings potential of up to $1000 per year. The message here is: Do not give up your day job. Naturally, any sales income will be dependent upon the author's individual marketing efforts, strategies and technique. Successful sales are also primarily based on a well-written book while being listed in a top-selling category.

The Hindu/Buddhist word "Karma" refers to the sum of effort/energy of one's actions in relation to a firm belief of your unique sense of power (as new authors) having no limits. You will also play an integral part among the global literary market and movement. All success/failure depends upon the time and effort you are willing to put forth. Karma also refers to the sum of effort/energy of one's actions in relation to his/her fate in future existences. Yet another Life lesson in self-belief.

Whenever you feel the moment is right; take control in influencing all of those upcoming/potential future readers. Whether by website/blog/social media personal/business page, take advantage of your book launch announcement with teasers/excerpts and even free giveaways to create a buzz. When asking friends/family to share your book details, don't be surprised how far word can travel in anticipation of the upcoming release date.

Social media content marketing and advertising remain among the top three revenue drivers for independent/self-published authors. Our potential as authors knows no limits so **BE** a force to be reckoned with. You will never find out unless you try.

Places where you can promote for FREE:
- Participate in a local/online podcast interview
- Create a YouTube channel/vlog
- Develop your own podcast
- Go on a local book tour/local authors
- Post on your blog/guest blog
- Initiate mailing lists
- Social media posts/release teasers/chapters
- Local media outlets
- Connect with local community/target readers
- Check out your local Toastmasters to talk up your book

As you begin your promotional journey of many twists and turns, you may at times feel like you're stuck in an "Alice in Wonderland" maze. At each dead end or negative/non response via phone, email etc., let it go and move on towards your next intended target. Feedback comes and goes but remain patient as positive reviews will soon appear on the horizon.

I would love to share one of my all time favorite books called The Four Agreements by a very wise Toltec (Mexican) author called Don Miguel Ruiz. Whenever you adhere to the following four Agreements in everyday Life and along your literary quest; you are sure to capture some Amazing experiences.

The Four Agreements:
1. Be Impeccable with your word
Present your very best finished book: well-edited with a captivating title, book cover and contents. Whenever discussing your book, speak with Pride and Gratitude.

Part Three: Let the Promotions Begin

Most of all, INSPIRE your readers and they will in turn feel your Positive Energy.

2. Don't take anything Personally
Take criticism/reviews with a grain of salt. Strangers do not know anything about you as you in turn, remain clueless to the daily life battles they may face. Remember there will be many more positive rather than negative reactions to come.

3. Don't' make Assumptions
When you keep expectations low, you will always be pleasantly surprised on a regular basis. Stay open to all blessings that come your way, continuously grateful for your literary accomplishments thus far.

4. Always Do your Best
You are Good Enough/ready to compete with all fellow writers out there. BELIEVE in yourself/your book and loyal readers will soon follow.

Throughout the process of writing this book, I came to realize just how much the Four Agreements relate to the overall creative process of a self-published book. In the big picture, it is imperative to stay True to you/your lovely book and never give up Hope. Keep the faith by dedicating valuable time to your marketing research and as you slowly chip away towards your goal, positive results will start to come.

On that note, let's now get started on this new and exciting Promotional quest. First of all, why not venture out and approach your local area libraries, bookstores, book clubs, media outlets etc. If your town/city newspaper prints a Features/Books section, contact the journalist/s before your book release. You might even get interviewed for an upcoming story so take that chance to shine. Local authors are usually well supported within their community as it comes as a welcome change from the same old run of the mill, national bestsellers.

Explore contact details for new book acquisitions

among local libraries/bookshops and arrange to drop off a complimentary book copy. Throughout the process, you may even make a good impression on the manager/owner who could consider you for a future event. Author talks/book signings will require practicing your public speaking skills as you are the one to best market your book. If chosen to be invited as a participant, take into account that speaking from the heart will always resonate with any audience.

Local schools and book clubs might also prove a great fit for your book, depending on your selected genre. The adventure is all yours for the taking. Select the venues that best suit your ideas/intentions.

Establishing an adjustable **budget** for your book marketing plan will be beneficial in the long run. During the design process for your book cover, it is advisable to create some of the following additional marketing materials:
- Business cards with book title, design, website etc.
- Bookmarks (complimentary with each book sale)
- Book flyers for author/book events
- Book poster board and stand (book cover/summary)
- Book Blurb (book cover, summary & website to add to promo emails)

Compare price rates with local printing companies while shopping around for the best prices. Although this adds to those initial costly expenses, having book materials/supplies on hand will assist greatly with in person sales/events. A sample order might consist of @ 250 business cards, bookmarks and flyers. An initial book order of 50+ books from your publisher is a great start. Take into account that ordering your book from the publisher will usually cost @ $5 or less per copy (at least half of your retail price). *Take note that whenever you place orders from the publisher, expect a much slower shipping/delivery

Part Three: Let the Promotions Begin

turnaround (one to two weeks on average).

Be prepared to give away/donate multiple books in order to create interest/future readers but only give from your heart (without expectation) or not at all. Set your personal budgetary limits as unexpected expenses will almost certainly arise. Ensure those extra expenses never cut into your household budget and remember why it was you wrote in the first place.

Hosting/sharing a stall at a local arts fair/market could be beneficial in getting known in your local community. In addition, library visits in your town, city, county, and state/province will always have you discovering many new outlets. Some libraries may even compensate you in appreciation for the extra patron attendance that your event creates. This welcome income always helps with incurred travel expenses, so why not combine your visit with a fun mini-getaway? You will soon become culturally enriched, leaving your comfort zone to discover new/unknown local destinations.

Perhaps you already host a website or social media page with dedicated followers where you could sell your book and create monthly giveaways/contests. This would be an appropriate time to begin accumulating those all important book reviews. On the promise of feedback, you might gift additional books for a limited time. Some authors give away book freebies in exchange for a posted Amazon/Good reads review. However, be prudent with your requests; I recommend no more than three appeals.

Bear in mind how much our daily lives are consumed with endless solicitations for product/services reviews. In addition, if readers enjoy your book, they will generally follow through with a review. Accumulating a minimum of ten book reviews is a pretty good start. Be aware most negative feedback will mainly emanate from unfulfilled keyboard warriors and trolls. Spoken from personal experience! In all honesty, try your utmost not to take negative comments personally and you will be just fine.

Lastly and most importantly, remind yourself: it isn't about the sales/comments but more on the lasting impact that your literary creation is having on the reading world.

"Nothing that's worthwhile is ever easy. Remember that."
–Nicholas Sparks

Part Three: Let The Promotions Begin
Chapter 2: How to Get Noticed Online

"Most obstacles melt away when we make up our minds to walk boldly through them."
                                    –Orison Swett Marden

In preparation for your initial email blitz campaign, it is wise to keep all contact details close at hand. If familiar with Microsoft Excel, why not create a spreadsheet where you can keep track of dates messages are sent/received. The old-fashioned way of ticking off addresses as you go also works fine. Staying on track often prevents annoying duplicate requests to potential interested parties. This way, you can start off your day in an organized and positive way.

Your unique book blurb helps to create an innovative email opener as far as attracting attention towards your new book. An appropriate size should just about cover the top part of the page while catching the eye of the recipient. Your message can begin just below your colorful and informative blurb.

*A **blurb** can be a short descriptive summary of your book. It should both attract/intrigue the reader into wanting to know more. Remember to include a book image along with a few catchy phrases.

The next important step would be to tailor a general introductory message specific to each of your intended email recipients. Take for example; public and academic libraries, bookstores/retailers, news media and so on. Communications with podcasts, book clubs, schools and institutions etc. should also consist of individual uniform requests. It will make your mail folders much easier to organize and work with on a regular basis. You can always personalize/update them at any time to conform to any marketing campaign.

A sample introduction towards targeting a notable potential book influencer might include the following:

"I have been a longtime fan of your work and would love to present you with a complimentary copy of my latest book based on….. I appreciate your time in reading my message……"

Introduce yourself, use flattery (usually works), recognizing similar traits to create a connection with your recipient. Book influencers often present themselves as great book followers.

Bookstagram is basically a booklover's paradise featuring a collection of artistically composed photos of books. Posts on these accounts often include book reviews, reading suggestions and book clubs to follow. Among some of the well-known book influencers are Michelle Reads Books, The Reading Women, Book Girl Magic and Reese Witherspoon's Book Club (1.5 million followers).

Twitter can become an effective way in communicating with the reading community while attracting new followers. If you happen to have a Twitter account, why not follow authors you like and learn from their tweets/comments on how they attract ongoing readership.

*On your social media accounts, copy and paste a recent five-star review along with a book teaser/excerpt/link and ask friends to share it.

Pinterest could be the perfect site to showcase your book cover and gain traffic towards your blog or website. It is a site designed to create image boards of recipes, art and decorative design ideas as well as inspirational quotes from writers.

Medium is a $5 membership website where

Part Three: Let the Promotions Begin 67

authors can publish individual posts or contribute to a publication, while getting paid. As an example, one post might attract @ 5000 views accumulating a possible $100 payment. The vast majority of subscribed writers generally publish one to two articles per month.

Substack is a free website for writers posting on a more regular basis who are paid directly by subscribers/readers. This allows for more of a direct relationship between writer/reader where the writer owns his/her individual IP/mailing list. Independent journalists often use this platform to thrive without having to follow all the ridiculous (free speech?) social media rules. You can even start up a paid newsletter on this site and keep up to ninety per cent of your revenue.

It is a good idea to target one library/district at a time, as chain emails are mainly considered spam. Although it may appear helpful at first to research names of library contacts, take note that individual may no longer be employed/has retired. Once you touch base with the exact individual, your connection can commence. Library directors/assistants/departments are often overwhelmed with tons of author requests (like yours) in daily inboxes, more than half of which end up in spam folders. How can your message be prevented from becoming a spam statistic? Well, let's talk about that....

Along with your blurb, the opening of your initial warm/polite email offers a brief introduction and reason for contact. Continue to create a buzz on innovative ways their readers would appreciate your new book. Work to your advantage using any online/professional reviews to attract additional interest. A Kirkus Review for example, @ $400+ is highly recognized in the literary field around the world. A couple of links should suffice within the body of your email. Avoid attaching files (unless requested) as most servers are armed with virus-protecting malware. Limit your message to one page, closing with a friendly offer of future additional details if needed. Always respond in kind whenever a library contact takes precious time to message you back, as your email obviously made a unique impact. Remind yourself of all the energy placed into your writing; this is the golden opportunity to sell your heartfelt effort to the world!

Throughout this entire process, realize that promoting you/your book will involve a communicative and dedicated process of drawing in new readers/retailers. This is going to take some time: **BE PATIENT**. You will always attract the right responses in time; be **KIND** to yourself and allow the process to take shape. Also, reflect on how preoccupied your recipient/s is at this time with a multitude of similar messages.
If one of your primary goals is to get your book noticed on **AMAZON** (let's be honest, it is hugely popular for readers/writers), these are some important tips to take into consideration.

- Create/update your **AUTHOR CENTRAL** account where you get to personalize and detail your book information. Upload your photo/s, website, blog and other pertinent notes. Reviewing similar authors in your genre will help entice your individual page toward readers about you/your wonderful book/s. This is the page where you really get to make it shine!

- **Goodreads Author Program** (owned by Amazon) is worth the free membership as yet another outlet engaging new readers towards your book. With over a million dedicated members, you are sure to garner some extra attention. Any review that posts on Amazon will also show up on the Goodreads site. This is primarily a reader-generated platform where authors like you can create a loyal following. There are also book giveaways that you can avail of during a dedicated time period but are not free of charge. As of 2021, it will cost you @ $119 to do so.

Linking your paperback and eBook (hardcover/Audible) also becomes an added advantage on **AMAZON**

Part Three: Let the Promotions Begin 69

while offering an additional reading choice. If you decide to create an audible version later, you add another option and readers/consumers LOVE extra reading options. The following website called **Booknook.biz** is an amazing resource for eBook conversions even for the most complex manuscripts, PDF's, books, interior layouts, Text, Word, Open Office Writer, Pages (MAC) etc. In return for a decent price, you will receive your very own MOBI and ePUB separate files for future marketing purposes. Check them out; you won't be disappointed. Spoken from personal experience and I will be using them again with this book. I keep the downloadable file for future use with additional online eBook distributors around the world.

Apart from Amazon book promotions, there are over two hundred online marketing platforms at your disposal. Tread carefully as piracy is big business in the self-publishing market; avoid wasting un-necessary expenses by doing your own online research. You will be grateful for the time invested before pressing forward with unwanted and unnecessary costly services.

Prior to paying for an online book marketing service, do extensive research, check reviews, pros and cons etc. Some may charge a fee while others require a monthly subscription service which can be cancelled at any time. If you pay the cheaper annual amount, be aware that it may take some time to receive a refund after you decide to cancel it.

There are some reputable publishing websites where you pay one small annual charge and can receive discounts on multiple publishing outlets/events.

ALLI – Alliance of Independent Authors is a global non-profit association for self-publishing authors. For an annual fee of @ $60, you can gain access to their author member forum, receive discounts and deals on multiple related sites, helpful monthly newsletters etc. Alli also acts as a watchdog for publishing companies who might try to rip you off, while providing expert tips on a range of publishing/marketing ideas. Try it for a year as you will at most; gain a wealth of informed insights to the literary world. Take full advantage of monthly informative emails on upcoming online classes/forums/book fairs and much more. www.allianceindependentauthors.org

Ibpa is an association of independent book publishers dedicated to professionalism and excellence. IBPA makes it easier for independent publishers to navigate the sometimes intimidating publishing process with over sixty unique member benefits. The annual fee is @ $110 with an additional $50 for an international subscription. www.ibpa-online.gov

"There are two ways of spreading light: to be the candle or the mirror that reflects it."
–Edith Wharton

Part Three: Let The Promotions Begin
Chapter 3: All About That Ego

"Don't worry about looking good; worry about achieving your goal."

- Ray Dalio

"How many books have you sold?" Prepare yourself for this intrusive question arising from enquiring minds of family, friends and even strangers. Now that you have catapulted yourself to the esteemed status of published author; you just might find yourself under the scrutiny of ongoing book successes/failures. Don't despair, as this line of questioning tends to dissipate after the novelty of your book launch is over.

There will always be those individuals who shy away from chasing their own dreams, choosing instead to live vicariously through the trials and triumphs of others. It's so much easier (lazier) to follow rather than lead, especially in the event you might make mistakes along the way. In which case, of course the onus will rest on you. On the contrary, you are the bold one; brave enough to have ventured into the literary unknown, in pursuit of one of your Life Dreams.

Whenever you reply to those nosey queries, your response can include: "To be honest, I have been so busy promoting my book that I haven't had time to focus on sales numbers at this point!" or your own brilliantly-contrived answer. The real truth is you will never know the exact number of books sold around the world. Chances are your book will be available on so many online platforms and eventually on second-hand book sites like Thrift Books, Powell's, The Strand, Book Mooch,

Skyo, Alibris, eBay etc. That by itself is pretty awesome, wouldn't you say?

If you decided to write a book primarily based on earning potential alone, you could be in for a rude awakening. Unless you happen to be a celebrity, established entrepreneur, You Tuber or social media sensation etc., those sales may take a while. Otherwise, get ready to motivate yourself towards countless diligent and dedicated long hours of hard work. The more time and energy devoted will be compensated in surprising ways, as long as you never abandon your goal.

Suppose you only sell about one hundred copies or less; you should still feel immense Pride on your achievement in publishing your book. You said you were going to do it and you did! From this moment forwards, all future goals and accomplishments will rest entirely on your shoulders as to how near/far you are willing to go. You are free to give it as little or as much time as you decide.

Guess what: you are/will be your very own personal promoter and publicist in every way that matters. That old saying of: "If you want something done right, you need to do it yourself!" will be pivotal at this stage. All future successes, whether in spurts or leaps will depend entirely on your earnest dedication and effort. There will undoubtedly be days when you might feel drained of any creative energy and contemplate giving up. However, the morning after, you could open an uplifting message in your inbox from a library wishing to purchase your book. If you concentrate on the positive rather than negative feedback; I guarantee a more balanced journey towards promoting your cherished book.

Ego tends to unleash an added hyper-sensitivity when it comes down to publishing your book. No doubt, it also relates to every author on the planet who has published literary works. Nothing can ever compare to clasping that created masterpiece in the palm of

Part Three: Let the Promotions Begin   73

your hands for the very first time. What an incredible achievement for a newly-published author; how can one's very ego not be heightened to a certain degree? Celebrate; perhaps toasting with a glass of champagne, take a deep breath and move on. There will be many uphill battles ahead, all of which will prove so worthwhile in the end.

    This may be the perfect moment to check that Ego at the door and park it there; otherwise, it may cause trouble along the book rollercoaster circuit you have chosen to embark upon. Stay true to the person you were before your book, without allowing any outside influence to alter your peace of mind. Nobody but you knows your story, background, challenges or the incredible efforts involved in writing this book. Do you have any idea how many people in the world have thought about writing a book but never get around to doing it; you have actually pushed through and accomplished what you set out to do.

    If by chance, you encounter an individual who name-drops and what they could do for you/your book and blah, blah, blah…take it all with a grain of salt. Unfortunately, there are a lot of people who are just talkers and don't follow up on promises. This, my friend; you are about to find out for yourself. Ego likes to rear its ugly head in the form of flattery, so choose wisely who to associate your beautiful book with as you may end up worse than before. In the end, isn't it more satisfying to do all the hard work by yourself?

    Always remember, flattery like happiness comes and goes, but self-confidence and contentment are not only more attainable, but elevate you to a better state of mind. That initial positive review may recall childhood/ school memories of being awarded the infamous gold star sticker, with you walking on air/sunshine. Just hold on long enough though, as a sneaky negative comment may soon appear in attempts to knock you off that pedestal perch. Not to worry, it's all part of this shiny and new inconspicuous author domain.

Since you've chosen to place yourself into the spotlight, the time now is to either take a bow or shy away. Coming this far; it's either go Big or go home. To serve as a reminder, this vital book feedback not only helps to keep your feet firmly grounded but also prepares you for the long path ahead. It might take some time but you will eventually veer towards the direction your book is meant to go. You've got this; look how far you have already come.

By now, you are beginning to understand just how the world of entertainment works. Place yourself in the shoes of entertainers who are often judged upon their latest song/movie releases. Imagine as they anxiously await dreaded do or die reviews with baited breath. Talk about Ego here; careers can be launched/ended solely based on public/press reactions. Be grateful this is not a part of your everyday world. Can you picture walking on eggshells every time you do something new?

Do me a favor and give yourself a break whenever you pause upon a review infused with a negative tone. As a reminder; every person who reads your book will have their own unique experience, with the mass majority posting positive feedback. Secondly, those not so kind words can occasionally expose book errors you were completely unaware of. (That's constructive help, right?) If you can move beyond taking them personally, you will not feel only enlightened but continue to excel as a writer/individual. Yes of course, it feels like an attack but eventually, you will reach the conclusion that your writing has touched countless readers in many positive ways.

In light of all of that outside influence, the old Ricky Nelson 1972 song "Garden Party" often comes to mind with the following chorus line:

Part Three: Let the Promotions Begin 75

"But it's alright now
I learned my lesson well
You see you can't please everyone
So you got to please yourself"

*<u>Please yourself</u> you always must, with this entire journey down to you and you alone.

Now, with all that initial feedback out of the way, perhaps with a minimum of ten plus reviews, how about reaching out for even more? It's not about being greedy at all as every single review helps you along the way. Nowadays, since each product/service revolves around obtaining feedback; why shouldn't it be the same for your book? Although it often feels like pulling teeth in repeat review requests, remember how busy life can be in our crazy interactive world. Remain patient in allowing your recipients plenty of time to post that coveted book review. Yes, it would be a perfect world if people always say what they mean, mean what they say and follow through but... C'est La Vie....such is Life. Unfortunately, not everyone has integrity.

It's important to know that there are generally two types of book reviews to become familiar with; crowd-sourced or professional. Let's dive in to find out more, shall we?

<u>Crowd-sourced reviews</u> will arise from everyday readers via Amazon, Goodreads, social media, blogs, websites, email reading lists and more. If you already have a solid social media presence, you're already halfway there. Why not create additional interest by hosting book giveaways and contests, while politely petitioning for a review (a positive one....just kidding!) or have trusted friends share your upcoming book launch on their pages. Word of mouth is always among the best referrals; proving such a trustworthy source.

Reviews will show up in spontaneous ways, mostly giving prospective readers an all round synopsis of your book and more importantly, whether to purchase it or not. As a reminder, every reviewer will incorporate their own unique interpretation, making it crucial for you to never take comments personally. By far, this is the speediest way to not only accumulate additional book sales but also ranks your book at a higher level towards getting known in the literary world.

The added advantage is that all of these reviews are FREE!

*Although crowd-sourced reviews will always raise your book's status, they are not used as a credible source by libraries or retailers.

Professional reviews will always resonate more with literary bases such as Kirkus, Publishers Weekly, Library Journal, Booklist, New York Times, US Review of Books, and BlueInk Review etc. It's a good thing that these types of reviews will never affect your Amazon or online book ranking but do carry a higher status.

A professional reviewer often tends to be an expert within your chosen book genre, experienced in providing an extensive summary of your written treasure. This educated reviewer (teacher, professor etc.) may also maintain a solid background and knowledge on the professional craft of book writing. Such trade publication reviews are highly relied upon by online retailers/libraries around the world.

Sadly though, only one person is providing you with a review, based on their individual opinion and style which may/not coincide with yours. However, this will prove to be a thorough and more detailed review, mostly articulating all aspects of your book/storyline. It doesn't hurt to purchase one professional review as you have nothing to lose and can always use it to your full advantage in promotional output. Why not be tenacious here; spend and live a little…You never know where it might lead.

*Expect to pay anywhere from $100-$600 for a

Part Three: Let the Promotions Begin

professional book review. Shop around and check reviews for the best experience possible.

Crowd-sourced or professional; you should take full advantage of these necessary and combined reviews as part of ongoing book-marketing materials. Including them in the body of emails, letters, fliers, sell-sheets or blurbs, you get to tailor quotes that will only further enhance solicitations to libraries, booksellers and the like.

Advantages of book reviews:
1. Confidence booster (Don't take things personally)
2. Valuable marketing tool (Use in metadata, website, social media, add review excerpts etc.)
3. Improve your writing skills (Learn from mistakes, revised editor, and elevate writing level)
4. Use for future book launch/es (Book series, future edition)
5. View the literary (reading) world more clearly

Browse the web for **Crowd-sourced reviews** that will cost less in the long run. The following are some examples to try. Some are free, while others are not. Check out each site's unique submission guidelines.

Here are some of the **FREE** ones:
- Amazon & Goodreads
- American Book Review
- Barnes & Noble
- Compulsive Reader
- Rain Taxi Review of Books
- Affaire de Coeur
- Booklife by Publishers Weekly
- Compulsive Reader
- The Rumpus

Here are some **fee-based** ones:
- Book Sirens ($10 sign-up/$2 per reader/possible review - Fiction only)
- Net Galley ($450 for 6 month subscription)
- Pubby (Free for 10 days/$20 per month)

78 HOW TO PROMOTE THAT BOOK YOU WROTE

- PR ($69 review package)
- Best Thrillers ($99 package)
- Fiverr (Graphic designers/book reviews etc.)

Book blogger websites sampling for additional reviews:
- Totally Bex (Romance)
- Literary Quicksand (International female authors)
- Geeky Galaxy (Science Fiction, Fantasy etc.)
- Reader Voracious (Fantasy, Horror, Sci-Fi etc.)
- Kelly Schuknecht (Fiction & Nonfiction)
- What Jamie Read (Children's, Diverse etc.)

There are a plethora of free/paid online book review sites out there to suit every budget and taste. Take your time to research/choose the one/s you like the best.

Most of all, allow this Review Rollercoaster to elevate you and your writing to new and exciting heights and never, ever let **EGO** get in the way!

"Our greatest glory is in never failing, but in rising every time we fall."
–Confucius

Part Three:
Let The Promotions Begin
Chapter 4: Slow & Steady Wins the Race

"The size of your success is measured by the strength of your desire, the size of your dream and how you handle disappointment along the way."
—Robert Kiyosaki

At this stage along your self-published book journey, you have most likely experienced highs and lows but see the value that dedication plays upon literary success. In the beginning, feeling rushed in your desire to become known as a new author, you now realize there is ample time to share your written work to the world.

Consider the race between the tortoise and the hare and on how the tortoise beats the hare every single time. Why is that? Well, according to Duke University researchers, the winner of the race always goes to the slower, steadier animal/participant. Over the space of a lifetime, it was discovered even the world's fastest animals become the slowest when their movements are averaged out, giving credence to Aesop's fable "The Tortoise and the Hare." The hare often became distracted in the story while the tortoise remained focused and steady.

The very same applies to you; a self-published author participating in a wondrous new world that began the very day your book went live. So many avenues for you to pursue without limitations, no matter where your confidence allows you to go rests entirely in your hands. Isn't that incredible that your penned creation has no end in sight, just filled with all your heartfelt energies?

Can you still remember when the internet was first introduced to the world and how overwhelming it felt signing on to AOL with "You've got mail" and "Goodbye"? (Those of us who dealt with those dial-up versions). Exciting, yet draining at the same time, we somehow adjusted to this innovative form of communication onto the wild, wild online west.

If you haven't had the time yet; arming yourself with a captivating sell-sheet will prove a useful tool along your marketing route. What exactly is a **sell-sheet**, you ask? Well, allow me to explain. It is a one-page book summary filled with important details that can further enhance your story. If done right, it illustrates your book metadata, compelling storyline, unique abilities/talents, marketing platforms, targeted readership and contact details.

Sample Sell-Sheet format:
- High-resolution book image
- About the book (brief summary/use compelling keywords)
- About the author (original yet catchy bio)
- Purchasing details: including book formats, ISBNs, pages, images, genre
- POD (Print on Demand) Publishers (discounts/return options-Ingram Spark only)
- Marketing (available online platforms, countries, etc.)
- Book recognition & awards/reviews
- Website and contact details/media/speaking engagements

Feel open to be original, yet detailed when creating your book sell-sheet to attract as much attention as possible. Similar to a resume, except the intention is to create higher future book sales etc. This sell-sheet can only aid a more profitable ad campaign, while attached to an introductory book message. Remember though, most

Part Three: Let the Promotions Begin

professional email recipients use spyware so it might be a good idea to ask first if it can be attached to a future email. You can always revamp your sell-sheet anytime as your book reaches new marketplaces.

Speaking of extra book marketing strategies; how far along are you in contacting library districts? Did you stay within the vicinity of your city, state or country? How about venturing further afield to new and exciting continents around the world? Check out some of the following websites for contact details for academic and public libraries across the globe:

www.worldcat.org
A collection of 15,637 libraries in 107 countries (OCLC member)

www.libraries.org
International library directory

www.ala.org
American Library Association

www.littlefreelibrary.org
A non-profit (based in Wisconsin) with mission to inspire readers/expand access to volunteer-led little free libraries around the world

www.usa.gov
Education/all libraries and archives

www.anythinklibraries.org
Colorado

Research and browse until your heart's content as there will always be a never ending supply of libraries where you can introduce your book. Compile organized lists according to city, county, state, country etc. Take your time in contacting targeted libraries, armed with all of those innovative marketing products. Whichever response you receive, make sure to express gratitude to the sender for taking such valuable time out of their busy day. Once again, taking notes of messages sent/received will save time in the long run as this can end up as a time-consuming but valuable endeavor.

It becomes a fun adventure sending/receiving messages from libraries in faraway lands, even if you've never left your own little part of the world. In a magical way, you/your book are making these trips, albeit via an online message. You will never know how far your little book can reach unless you try!

Another area where you can make an impact on future book sales would be with paid advertising on Amazon. Although Facebook, Twitter and Instagram can help somewhat, Amazon (Goodreads) is the place where millions of people around the world search for their next read. Similar to grocery shopping in your local supermarket, while spotting sales/promotions on similar products you already buy. On Amazon, where 60% of readers are constantly browsing for new books; if your title pops up on the screen as "sponsored/books you might like etc.", it just might result in a click/purchase. You will only get charged per click, which may/not turn into a sale….who knows unless you give it a shot. Starting off with a minimum of ten cents per click might not be a bad idea as you dip your toes in the Amazon advertising waters.

Prior to details on possible future clicks/sales, let's first do a little tidying up of your book/author page on Amazon. Here are some tips to make your book more appealing to prospective readers/buyers. Look at selling your book on Amazon etc. the same way as if you were getting ready to sell your house. You would do the utmost in order to attract the perfect buyer, right? Well, Amazon Central is a book marketing hub where both the author and

Part Three: Let the Promotions Begin

the reader can come together to create the perfect match. www.authorcentral.amazon.com

"Author Central is the place where authors can build their author stories – adding photos, editing their biography, building a bio and more. Because Author Central is designed for authors, we make it easy to find answers to questions about selling books on Amazon.com"

Once adding your book/to join, you may opt to receive/not author tips via email. You will then see a screen displaying your photo/book welcoming you to Author Central. Now take dedicated time to add/review/manage your book/s listed on Amazon and review where the updated sales rankings stand. Click on GO on your author page to view as it would appear to a potential customer/reader. From this point on, feel free to add/delete/change details at any future time.

How to make your Amazon Central book/author page SPARKLE:

1. Post professional-looking author headshots/photo/s (smiling is always good), up to 8 are allowed, including pets, hobbies etc. Feel free to also add up to 8 videos (max 10 minutes each)
2. About the Author: compose a charming biography that readers can relate with and follow, create additional links to mailing lists/book giveaways, recent podcasts etc.
3. All book/s will be listed here with possible teasers for future launch/es
4. Blogs/RSS Feeds – link your blog to Amazon Central while directing additional traffic to your online blog
5. Provide details on upcoming events/talks

Amazon book campaign Advertising

The introduction to Amazon Advertising launched in 2012 which in turn allowed authors and sellers all over the world to advertise their products.

Amazon book advertising campaign. This paid service is similar to a pay to play system where you will only be charged per book click (average of 81 cents). Of course, the cost is not set in stone as it all depends on your budgeted amount. Each individual book ad campaign (don't forget to name it) may begin with perhaps $5 per day (usually not spent) with say a maximum cap of $100. It may even take a few months or more until your budget is spent/clicks made. 10 cents per click is a good place to start out.

Once your book is enrolled in KDP www.kdp.amazon.com, log on, go to your dashboard, click on bookshelf and then on the Promote and Advertise link. From here, you can set up all new advertising campaigns and check on them regularly. Review all the accepted guidelines before you begin. For a more thorough understanding of how to proceed, check out the following website for helpful tips.

www.evergreenauthors.com

According to multiple authors who have used Amazon advertising, their general assessment is: "Right now, using Amazon advertising to sell your book is pretty profitable. There isn't much competition; therefore the cost per click is pretty low. This simple system can help you Revive a book of yours that isn't making sales."

Take note that there are basically two types of advertising available to the author; **Sponsored Products** or **Product Display** ads:

-**Sponsored Product** ads will appear as part of the search results/product details pages. These pages show up based on specific keywords. (Imperative to have genre specific keywords to attract interested readers)

-**Product Display** ads will appear on product detailed related pages as well as on some Kindle home screens by way of a screensaver. These concentrate more on products related to your book. To decide which one will work best for

Part Three: Let the Promotions Begin

you, check out the differences between the two options.
    Although there are many decisions to be made along this steady and often frustrating journey, always remind yourself that everything rests in your very own capable hands. You alone are the Captain of this book's course with the ability to steer it in the direction of your choice. Should you encounter rocky waters, (which you inevitably will) alter your sails for a safe return home.

"I can't change the direction of the wind, but I can adjust my sails to always reach my destination."
–Jimmy Dean

Part Three:
Let the Promotions Begin
Chapter Five: Never Give Up!

"Never bend your head. Always hold it high. Look the world straight in the eye."
— Helen Keller

Never stop BELIEVING in this Amazing Literary Journey you ventured upon all by yourself. The countless high and low moments (definitely more highs) will continue on for as long as you "soldier on" with this mission of a lifetime. You alone get to decide how much/little dedicated time to invest.

    Ignore all the "naysayers" as they really possess nothing more than negative/envious energies; instead remain steadfast to all the positive minds you have connected with thus far. Affirmative feedback, encouragement and goodwill will always keep you grounded to advance along this chosen path.

    Imagine if you had ignored that inner voice, discarded the idea of writing a book, not to mention realizing your dream? You just might be living with immense regret right now. However, look at the outcome; thanks to you, your book is not only completed but published in a physical book! Can you even grasp what an exemplary role model you have become for all aspiring writers contemplating a future book in the making? If nothing else, that notion should gift you with the deepest fulfillment.

    Permit me to share the following success stories about everyday authors whose books were developed into a movie. When a particular storyline touches the hearts and minds of so many readers; who can say it

Part Three: Let the Promotions Begin

might also one day become a screenplay/movie? The majority of movie-goers are often unaware that the compelling movie they're engaged in actually had a simple beginning as an ordinary fiction/nonfiction book.

Take for example, the moving tale of "Still Alice" by novelist/neuroscientist Lisa Genova and the toll Alzheimer's disease took on her family. Although strongly advised by a book agent not to publish such a sad story as it could lead to a "career-killer", she pressed on to self-publish the book, primarily selling it out of the trunk of her car. Creating a buzz on MySpace, Goodreads etc. and book-signing events, she eventually invested in a Public Relations agent and the rest, as they say is history. It went on to become a 2015 hit movie with Julianne Moore starring in the main role of Alice and attracted much needed attention to the ongoing plight of Dementia and Alzheimer's on our society.

An additional range of books converted to recent Netflix hits include the following titles:
- One Hundred Years of Solitude by Gabriel Garcia Marquez
- Shadow and Bone by Leigh Bardugo
- Carrie Pilby by Caren Lissner
- The Woman in the Window by A.J. Finn
- Maid by Stephanie Land
- You by Caroline Kepnes
- Bridgerton by Julia Quinn
- The Queen's Gambit by Scott Frank

Countless authors would love nothing more than to witness their original book transformed into an onscreen movie. But how would one go about it? In all honesty, it is likely time-consuming as it involves sending a manuscript to multiple literary agents. A writer should be prepared for many rejections, trying not to take them personally (easier said than done). Nonetheless, if you never give up, one fine day you just might acquire a book contract with the right agency/producer/screenwriter. These book rights are generally attained for one year at around $5,000 after which you are notified if a project (option) is indeed in the works/not. Bear in mind, it may take several years until the perfect connection/combination can be realized. Just ask Caren Lissner of "Carrie Pilby". She endured the full spectrum with her book being optioned three times before finally becoming a hit movie starring Gabriel Byrne. Check out her story here @ www.tingcooperative.com

    Have you ever heard of a **Universal booklink (UBL)**? No, well let me explain another wondrous example as a result of all that dedicated hard work you've undergone in marketing/promoting your book. This is a link that directs the reader to a web page illustrating all the sites carrying your wonderful book/eBook/audio book. When the user clicks on any of the images, it takes them directly to their preferred websites like Amazon, Barnes & Noble, WH Smith, Wal-Mart, etc. where they can purchase a book copy. Isn't that all due to your Amazing effort on never giving up on your goal to reach more readers everywhere?

    Now, let me show you how to make your amazing book **UBL (book link)** to share with the world. One of the easier sites to create this on is via www.draft2digital.com Since 2016, with their introduction of Books2Read, authors have access to many additional tools and resources for book marketing. Once your book/s are set up with Draft2Digital/Books2Read, all you have to do is copy your URL (your online book link), then paste that link into the Universal Link generator. Then, click on the "Make my Universal Link" button and voila! Now, you can use this precious, professional link with all future outgoing marketing messages. Isn't that incredible? Lastly, don't forget to add all the additional sites where your book title has recently become available.

    Throughout your ongoing book experiences, try to

Part Three: Let the Promotions Begin

remember The Four Agreements (Don Miguel Ruiz) and as long as you...
1. Be Impeccable with your word
2. Don't make assumptions
3. Don't take things personally
4. Always Do your Best

You will be well on your way to becoming a memorable author.

One of these fine days, when you get to feeling down or are perhaps having a Murphy's Law day; why not Google your name/book title? You just might feel your heart soar as you witness all your hard effort on display for the world to see. Remember that local podcast, library visit, newspaper story, blog post and so many more events you took part in but perhaps have forgotten? Check out the hundreds of libraries, retailers and places around the world that now stock your beloved book.
All of this, my fellow author is down to your diehard dedication in NEVER GIVING UP! You did it! Be PROUD of all that you have accomplished so far, with so many more opportunities to come. You can continue to take your book/s anywhere you wish....

"To thine own self be true, And it must follow, as the night the day, Thou canst not then to be false to any man."
- William Shakespeare/Hamlet

Part Four: Tales From A Self-Published Author
Chapter 1: Celtic Road Home to America

"Between saying and doing, many a pair of shoes is worn out."
- Iris Murdoch

Running away from home (Dublin, Ireland) at the naïve and tender age of eighteen introduced me to an excitingly, scary new world yet to be discovered. Although many dark times lay ahead, possessing both an optimistic and curious mind somehow always managed to get me through. Surviving London for two brief months also took me back in time to my father's arrival there in 1949 and how he had been treated as an inferior Paddy/Irishman. Early on, deciding that we were living different lives in different times; I would not allow racial ignorance get in the way of my future Life Dreams.

It was mid summer of 1981 and the infamous wedding of Charles and Diana was about to take place. London was abuzz with an uplifting pride of the royals with emblematic souvenirs adorning windows and doorways as far as the eye could see. Mere weeks later however, all was done and dusted as nearby street vendors along with the rest of London carried on about their business. Had it even taken place?

Within a short time span, three job offers came my way including, reservationist at the upscale Hotel Bristol in Mayfair, breathalyzer tester at Bow Street Police Station (beside The Old Bailey Courthouse) and lastly, a handbag factory position in Barbican. Opting for the hotel

Part Four: Tales From A Self-Published Author

Celtic Road Home
Book Cover

Dublin on Celtic Cross

position, I lasted three days before quitting in tears on a rainy afternoon (talk about downpours), soon deciding London was not going to work out after all. It had felt cold and unwelcoming from the start.

St. Louise Hostel in Westminster became my living arrangements for the entirety of the brief London stay, where I was delighted with a tiny, corner room with a sink. No bother, as it meant the existence of my very own unique living space. Sharing a communal kitchen (you guessed right; milk and food often went missing) with other young ladies created the opportunity for this Irish lass to go international. Besides practicing French with a couple of ladies from Lyons and Guadalupe, a young lawyer from Italy's fashion capital of Milan quickly caught my eye. To cut a long story short, it was Grazie (thanks) to Cinzia that initiated my London escape, bringing about an extraordinary twelve-year adventure (or as my dear old Mum would say "Gallivant") around Europe and beyond.

From 1981 to 1993, I made my home in London, Milan, Paris, Avignon, Rome, New York, Birmingham (UK), Alcala de Henares (Madrid), Palma de Mallorca and The Hague (Netherlands) before finally coming to America for good. Living in the USA had always been a dream of mine since early childhood days in Dublin. Besotted and glued to American TV shows since the early 1970s, I made a vow that someday, somehow my childhood Dream would come true.

Thanks to a blissful encounter with a southern gentleman and USAF veteran (my dear hubby Jimmie/ Captain Fox), reality hit in early March, 1993 in The Netherlands and the DREAM began in earnest.

The creative idea of writing a book had always lingered in the back of my mind but remained out of reach while raising my young son, Ryan. Over the years though, friends and acquaintances often commented on comical past adventures making a great book. Argh,

Part Four: Tales From A Self-Published Author

perhaps someday...

In early 2016, the time finally felt right to begin the lengthy book-writing process with many starts and stops along the way. Believe it or not, my comfortable writing space turned out to be on my bed. Complete with a dotted black and white wooden tray topped with a slowly-dying Dell lap top, firm pillows at my back, the book was slowly begun. Comfort turned into a necessity paired together with a quiet oasis for the creative process to take place. That is whenever the phone didn't ring/vibrate or daily interruptions took me away from the solitude of writing. Better days were ahead....

Upon the conclusion of each chapter, I would often subject my poor hubby to patiently listen while reading out loud. It actually became a really useful tool to catch common grammar mistakes, spelling etc. As he paid attention, often giggling at some of my crazy past life adventures, he anticipated the beginning of the upcoming chapter. He was curious to discover if I had again become homeless, jobless or was once again discovering a new country alone. What an unexpected gem he became throughout the entire writing process.

Feedback soon became a strong motivator in those early chapters emailed to close family and friends. Their reaction/guidance/support provided just the right energy needed to carry on. Sentences were transformed into paragraphs, pages into chapters and so on. This book was really starting to take shape. An unexpected addition of photos at the start of each chapter was the brainstorm of a fellow legal immigrant from Romania called Lili. She had loved the first three chapters, touching on how memoir readers would connect better if the book had photos included. Quickly gathering scores of past memories from old photo albums, I copied them to my phone and organized them into time-related images. Ask me today if they have all been returned to the correct place and you can probably guess the answer...!

Making the decision to write only when feeling inspired to do so really helped the chapters to flow together. The unexpected came, whenever I happened to be writing a chapter about a new city. It was as though I was transported back there in that time and place once again. All the characters and events slipped back into my mind's eye, as though decades gone by had been just mere moments in the recent past.

Towards reaching about three quarters of the way along the literary journey, everything came to a screeching halt. Suddenly, I had lost the plot and decided to let it sit for who knows how long. Somehow, all motivation and inspiration to write had left and it was only thanks to a dear friend that I could conjure up the energy to get to the end. Windy had just started a new gas station position, having tons of idle hours a day and was in search of additional reading materials. I quickly had the first nine of twelve chapters printed at the local UPS Store, reminding her of it still being a rough draft (no edits). I bundled the pages into a shoe box and off she cheerily went on a chilly October morning.

Windy called a week later, while engrossed in the captivating travel tales, cheekily asked for the next chapter. As I had explained earlier, it hadn't been written as of yet. Her response: "Well, c'mon sister, chop, chop!" What could I say, with no excuses left but to compose and finish the next chapter. The last two followed suit, anticipating a week later, I would once again be presented with the same request. Wow, without her supportive push, it may have taken months or years to reach the end of the book. All of us individually succumb to a level of procrastination (Ok Lazy) but boy, to be gifted with such support and belief is truly something to be extremely Grateful for....THANK YOU WINDY!

Towards late 2016, with the end of the book now in sight, it came time to study as much as possible about self-publishing for rookie authors like me. Multiple hours were spent tolling on websites, taking notes from a free Udemy course, YouTube as well as constant research on the entire subject matter. Moments of self-doubt would often creep in, asking myself: Are you crazy to think you can do this by yourself? Who do you think you are? Is this process too overwhelming? And yes, looking back on it all; it really felt like a battle. In contrast though, I had already survived so much in Life, twenty times harder in faraway lands, not even able to speak the language. So, heck yeah, I would and could most definitely do this!

In early January of 2017, researched notes firmly in place and a bold spring in my step, I quickly began the search for a talented graphic designer. On the third attempt, Sean Stennett was the obvious choice. The irony in that he lived near Dublin Blvd. wasn't a determining factor...Ha-ha! He was extremely talented in art and business logo design and listened to all my innovative thoughts. Brainstorming creative ideas together, we soon designed the perfect book cover for Celtic Road Home: A Memoir. What a fun and exhilarating time this is for any author; without a doubt among one of your best moments in book writing. Savor every single minute of it as it will demonstrate a hidden and creative side you didn't even know exists.

Sean soon developed into my go-to person in all aspects of preparing the book for self-publishing. Without his expertise, it would have taken my un-techie self unlimited time to design, format and upload, with so many stringent and specific requirements. What a Godsend he has been in my life...We all have our talents, which is why I always believe it best to leave certain jobs to the experts. Wouldn't you agree?

One day before the final book cover, formatted manuscript etc. was to be uploaded online, I sent the cover image to trusted family and friends for their input. Upon sight of the Celtic cross on the bottom right hand corner, my sister asked what meaning it had? I quickly responded that it represented Dublin, the place of my childhood. Thankfully, she noted that nobody would ever know that (without reading the book) since the cross could be a symbol of many Celtic cultures. Instantly, I messaged Sean asking if he could place the Celtic cross on the Dublin sign. It was quite late in the game with the design already set in stone, but maybe, just maybe there was a chance to change it?

    The following morning, Sean showed up, his faithful Mac laptop tucked under his arm and sat down at the kitchen table. As he began opening up his phone, he mentioned on his way over, he had taken a photo while at a stop light on Dublin Blvd. To my amazement, the street name was Celtic Cross Grove with Dublin as the cross street above. It was indeed a sign that all would be perfect with Dublin and the Celtic cross together. This would be the first of many miracles that would soon evolve from my little book. All I can say is that sometimes in Life; there are certain moments that are just meant to be. Without wondering why, we must accept to "Live" in the moment, safe in the knowledge our paths are already set. However, I believe that all Life Choices and their ultimate consequences are entirely up to us; ones which we will not only learn from, but also evolve.

    A month later, while attending a funeral for an old work colleague of my husband's at The Broadmoor Hotel, I was approached by their personal photographer. Mic was responsible for taking photos (Hall of Fame) of all visiting celebrities and had just done so with a recent stop by Arnold Schwarzenegger. As he had overheard me talking about my upcoming book, it would be an honor to take my photo for the cover. A few days later, I felt like a celebrity posing about by the hotel lake with Mr. Mic snapping away. The camera sounds reminded me of an early 1980s Duran Duran song called "Girls on Film". Later on though, choosing just one final photo from over

Part Four: Tales From A Self-Published Author

a hundred became just as time-consuming as the heavy book editing ahead. Talk about Luck of the Irish though!

All throughout the writing of my memoir, the title of "Celtic Journey" had deeply resonated into the storyline, easily making it a first choice. Nonetheless, after searching among similar titles one summer afternoon, I quickly got dismayed by a knitting pattern book of the same name. Ugh, what to do now? No worries, it wasn't long before "Celtic Road Home" came to light and problem solved. An original title really does make all the difference when the author wants to create an impact on the reading world. Wouldn't you think?

Following a few online searches, I lucked upon a fabulously, kooky lady called Hitch in Arizona who runs a website called www.booknook.biz Incredibly gifted in the publishing world, Hitch and her team graciously created my eBook in superfast response time. The reason for the rush was due to the fact I had recently called up a local Gazette reporter called Stephanie who had written an article on another local Colorado author. Might she take interest in my upcoming memoir about never giving up on getting to America? Turns out, after a chat with her editor (with immigration always a hot topic) we got the go ahead for a Sunday front page feature in the Life section on the same weekend after the Amazon launch.

The rush was now on to get it finished up despite my becoming a bit lazy and complacent. There's nothing like a deadline to push you into reaching the end goal.

March 7th of 2017 was the metamorphosis following a long period of incubated writing with the newly published book imitating a beautiful butterfly. As it turned out, it was also the fifth anniversary of my father's passing. Gerard Mary Doolan was also literary-inclined, having been the sole author/creator of his own patriotic newspaper called VICTORY back in the late 70s and early 80s. It felt as though he was not only watching over and inspiring my writing but was also immensely proud. It had also been, thanks to him that my world journey began!

It was so very important for me to have converted this Inspirational Celtic Journey into the written word. The original intention was to someday leave behind an uplifting Life lesson for my future grandchild/ren. As an unexpected bonus though, it actually turned out to become an Inspiring read that resonated with so many readers. That alone will always continue to warm my heart that other souls have been touched by mere words…

"You use a glass mirror to see your face: you use works of art to see your soul."
- George Bernard Shaw

Part Four: Tales From A Self-Published Author
Chapter 2: Starting Out Local

"It's lovely to know that the world can't interfere with the inside of your head."
- Frank McCourt/Angela's Ashes

The magical moment of cradling your newly-published physical book in your hands is one you will forever cherish. For me, it compares to the perfection of a newborn baby, following nine long months of anticipation and loving, self care. The toll of all that hard labor in creating this new book has now come to this moment in time. Now the hard work really begins as you nurture the stages of your book's journey from the launch date to infinity and beyond. Ok, I stole that from the Toy Story movie!

A few loyal friends on both sides of the Atlantic had purchased the book right on the release date, taking advantage of Amazon Prime's fast delivery. My own magical reaction would materialize just a few days later. Ryan, my adult son had stopped by, noticed it on a nearby table and remarked that it looked like a real book. "It is a real book!" came my joyous and proud response on having transformed an original idea into a glossy, colorful new book complete with nearly three hundred pages.

The first real step was to gain recognition in the local Pikes Peak Library District (PPLD) in Colorado Springs. The week before, I had found out about an annual event called "Mountain of Authors" where thirty local authors are selected among two hundred applicants to showcase their literary accomplishments. One of

HOW TO PROMOTE THAT BOOK YOU WROTE

Gazette "Signings & Such"

Perfect Pairing!

Part Four: Tales From A Self-Published Author

the afternoon sessions called "I've written a book; now what?" sounded interesting. To my surprise, I received a phone call from Bryan, the event organizer a couple days later with an invitation to participate. It also happened to be Saturday, April 1st – April Fool's Day. Skeptical at first, I told Bryan I had already planned on attending the afternoon session as an audience member. A library employee had dutifully informed me a week earlier that as a new author, it might be some time before I could score an invitation due to the volume of established authors in the local area.

It was then he mentioned one of the invited authors having to bow out at the last moment and would I like to be the replacement? Still in doubt, I had been informed that there was a waiting list of other authors. That was true but based on a recent newspaper story; they felt it was an interesting read leading to the invitation. That same Gazette article (instigated by yours truly) had also prompted a local reader to request the library district to purchase/stock my book. You really never know how one tenacious request can lead you/your book to future gigs. Always Believe that you can do it and you surely will...

What a thrilling April fool's Day it had turned out to be, after all. When reality suddenly hit that it was only one week away, I soon went into panic mode. At the event, of course I would get the chance to sell my book, but only had one solitary copy in my possession. The only alternative was to order ten copies at full price from Amazon as there was no way I was showing up without any books. In hindsight, when the book had been released two weeks earlier, it would have been smart to order twenty-five copies at the author/half price. Live and learn, as they say. Albeit with a slower delivery time, they might have arrived by now. As an added reminder, anytime you purchase your own book via Amazon at full or discounted price, take note that you are not eligible to earn sales royalties.

The following Saturday, April 8th arrived quickly and was a typically beautifully, sunny Colorado morning. Armed with books and Celtic-themed props, (thanks to recent sales at Party City/St. Patrick's Day two weeks prior) we arrived early to set up our author table complete with a crisp white tablecloth. Lunch was kindly provided as we all eagerly waited for the doors to open to the public. Meanwhile, it was great to mingle with fellow authors, some of whom were on their fifth, sixth books etc. The hours passed quickly in between listening to the panel of speakers (me excitedly taking valuable notes) with intermissions where our tables were visited by the general public and we sold a few books. At the end of the day, the library deducted a twenty per cent commission, while writing a check for the balance. A total of four books were sold which felt like a great first achievement.

It was quite interesting to observe three quarters of the audience raised hands when questioned who wanted to/was writing a book. As it turned out, there was such immense interest in the entire process; who knew it would one day prompt the writing of this self-guide book!

The second book promotion culminated with an appropriately titled annual weekend event in Colorado Springs called "Celtic Fest". It would take place in popular Memorial Park in mid-June, allowing plenty of time to order those author-priced books. Go big or go home as they say; so I really went to town creating flyers, business cards, bookmarks, poster board/book stand etc. Cost a fortune it did, not to mention the steep $440 for the weekend stint. With my heart ruling my head I thought, "Let's at least give it a try" as always, opting for the positive approach.

As it would turn out, my naive expectations took a bit of a beating. However, it was a fun weekend listening to all the Celtic bands play, the colorful kilts, tasty but expensive food/drink (Guinness) and banter with fellow vendors. Fun fact; the man at the next table could connect your Celtic last name/heritage to a colorful kilt and order it as part of a traditional family keepsake. Karen, on the other side bought the second copy of my book, and throughout the weekend became engrossed reading it which made it all worthwhile. I also got my first official outside customer called Lindsay who was a huge art lover and talented artist. Hey, you win some and you lose some, that's Life. I also got chatting with Martin, a fellow Dubliner (manager of Jack Quinn's downtown pub) and found myself (as you do around others from your childhood hometown) speaking with old slang words/sayings not voiced in decades. It's funny how you can become morphed into a totally different person just by your way of banter.

  The Bookman, a charming bookstore in Old Colorado City became the first to invite me to a book-signing on 21st August, 2017. That weekend happened to coincide with one of those rare lifetime events; a Total Solar Eclipse. Most interested parties had other weekend plans in mind, including driving north to Wyoming to witness more of an up close experience. A few regulars stopped by and browsed as part of their weekend activities. Some even approached my table by the door, perhaps intrigued by my Celtic tones. It also might have been a result of all my uplifting, positive or even solar energies! I actually ended up selling six copies to the unexpected surprise of our highly-literate hostess/vendor stating two or three was the norm for book-signing sales for a new author. Although it might take a while; I was going to give it my all it all along each step of the way.

  Another local nearby business in Old Colorado City called British Pantry invited me to host a book reading and cream tea. Maria (Brighton, England) and I had established a combo price for both, the result of which became a successful afternoon. While signing book copies, many a customer reminisced on past/upcoming travels to The Emerald Isle. A short while late, as Maria wrote out the final check, it gave rise to yet another achievement. This only served as additional motivation along this new literary path.

At this point, I had approached most of the bookstores in the area since springtime. The routine went as follows: 1) I would call to introduce myself as a local author, 2) find out the manager/owner's name, 3) request a convenient time to stop by with a complimentary book copy and, 4) ask if there might be the possibility for future book-signing events.

One Monday morning, being the only day of the week the owner was there, I followed the promotional ritual. Mary appeared as a super busy book lady but patiently listened to my book offer/request. Upon learning that I hailed from Ireland, she exclaimed: "We've just recently returned from our son's wedding at a castle in Doolin, Ireland!" I couldn't believe it, as my maiden name "Doolan" derives from that same area. What a serendipitous coincidence. Smiling, as I departed, I pictured my Dad giggling on the other side. Although it would take another year and a half, Mary and Joe Ciletti from "Hooked On Books" finally offered me a book-signing date just before Christmas 2019 and were delightful and kind hosts.

Towards late summer, my sister in-law Jayne had proposed the idea of creating an audio book, primarily in mind for blind readers to enjoy. The idea of audible books hadn't even crossed my mind. Nevertheless, the more thought I gave it in addition to the popularity of audio books, why not? Although, how much more would that add to an already overextended book budget? My husband often jokes that I will continue to be in the red (as far as income) for the next decade, lol!

Fortunately, after a steep $3000 price quote from a professional studio/radio station, I managed to locate a talented young sound/technical engineer called Jesse who lived just five minutes drive away. He operates Rewind

Part Four: Tales From A Self-Published Author

Records (on face book) straight out of his basement. Jesse had worked with many musicians, rappers etc., had never created an audio book before but was totally up for the challenge. Together, over a two-week period in early October, we managed to complete the audio book. They were two of the hardest weeks I had ever worked, having never used my voice on such a scale. Now, I finally understood what singers, DJ's, announcers and newscasters have to go through. You automatically believe your voice is always going to remain strong, until it isn't. Poor Jesse had to toll through so much editing (reducing an initial 30+ recording hours down to 14) that I believe my book would end up being his first and ultimately the last!

Apart from a few other local, supportive bookstores, the final two events for the year took place at local military installations. The first was on a Saturday in early December at Peterson AFB where I imagined Christmas shoppers stopping by for a Christmas gift idea. That turned into way too much positive expectation, on my part. Although I had purposefully chosen a table site near the entrance, most passersby carried on with such intent, (as I also do whenever I shop) heading directly to their destination. Let's face it; you want to get in and out as fast as you can when it comes to shopping, right? Ok, so I know being a tad more aggressive might have helped, but that's just not my style. Although, I did warmly wish most of the passersby a "Merry Christmas", it was the most I could muster. It ended up more trouble than it was worth with one lonely sale at the end of four hours. Following-up with a bureaucratic way of form-filling (I was on a government property)...need I say more. However, interesting conversation with a few wise souls/fellow vendors as well as female support from a couple of commissary employees/friends (Mariafe and Josie) ended the day on a high note. We were even pointed out to an elderly gentleman whose son happens to be a prime time soap opera leading actor.

The following Saturday sparked another four-hour session at Fort Carson Army base on the other side of town. As we parked, what I believed was a good omen seeing the Shamrock Foods truck (that's how my Dad greets me from the other side) delivering food just feet away. Once again, setting up a table right by the entrance felt like a welcome energy. Did I tell you that Army folk are super friendly and very down to earth to boot? I have always considered Air Force like the store Target and Army Wal-Mart. If you shop at both stores, then you know exactly what I'm talking about.

With the first hour having passed, I began to notice a group of people gathering nearby, wondering what/who they were waiting for. As it happened, a World War II veteran/Pearl Harbor survivor at the young age of 104 had just penned a memoir and was due to host a book event. In the following moments, a smiling, frail gentleman was briskly wheeled past followed by a body guard to a steady stream of applause. Wow, this must have been somebody really important who had fought for his country. In fact, James W. Downing had been commanding officer of the USS Patapsco during the attack on Pearl Harbor (December 7th, 1941) and the second oldest living survivor. As it turned out, his bravery in "Remember Pearl Harbor" was the reason for the adoring crowd and rightfully so. Just two months later on February 13th of 2018, this Amazing American Hero and war veteran passed away. What an honor to have shared space in such patriotic company on that Saturday in December, 2017. May you forever rest in Peace Commander Downing, member of "The Greatest Generation". Thank you, dear James for your devoted military service to America.

After a while, the crowd had begun to thin out with happy faces heading towards the exit with a signed copy of his book. Wow, some competition I was facing now or what? Every twenty minutes or so, the intercom would

Part Four: Tales From A Self-Published Author

announce this hero's presence/book event which got me to thinking: Could I get my book event mentioned also? Who did this feisty Irish lady think she was anyways? No, I had not fought in a world war, but hey, my book was an equally interesting read. With a spring in my step, I politely approached the store manager standing next to the veteran requesting a similar public address announcement, with the nearby bodyguard grinning at my audacity.

Be careful what you wish for as ten minutes later, after scribbling down a few author/book notes, there came an announcement for my book-signing too. Tenacity, if timed just right can often result in success or failure; how will you know unless you give it a try? Now; did it garner a bunch of book sales? Not if my life depended on it. However, I was once again Blessed with one lonely customer who was the son in-law of Stephanie, the Peterson Commissary produce manager. Stephanie had loved the complimentary copy I'd gifted her with over the summer and advised her son in-law what a great Christmas gift it would make for his wife. The poor man patiently waited as I struggled with a complicated Square online payment. After double-charging, I was finally able to correct it and issue him with a credit.

What an incredibly, busy nine months it had been since that early March. It felt as though I had run a few marathons but with no regrets. A brand new year would soon begin with more exciting and innovative book marketing ideas to come. Life was good.

"Be yourself, everyone else is already taken."
–Oscar Wilde

Part Four: Tales From A Self-Published Author
Chapter 3: Homeward (Dublin) Bound

"We are all in the gutter, but some of us are looking at the stars."

–Oscar Wilde

Early one morning in mid-November, 2017, I emailed an organization in Dublin called Creative Ireland. Established the year before to commemorate the hundredth anniversary of the Easter Rising of 1916, it would celebrate all Irish artists, both near and far from 2017 to 2022. In the message, I offered a brief summary on my Celtic Road Home to America, complete with a Fighting Irish Spirit. The email contents also included a blurb, website, links and reviews. As with all other emails; once the "sent" option was clicked, it was released without another thought. Remember; low to no expectations are the best. That way, you will always be pleasantly surprised whenever a reply magically shows up on your radar.

      Upon waking up the very next morning, not only was there a kind message from Clodagh (love that name) congratulating me on the book but that she had also forwarded the book details to Libraries Ireland. The second unexpected email came from Evelyn, Senior Librarian for Dublin City Libraries (DCL) with a surprising ten book order of "Celtic Road Home: A Memoir." Goodness, what an amazing turnaround from having reached out less than just twenty-four hours earlier. Along with the seven-hour time difference, both responses had landed in my mailbox in the middle of the night. This Celtic Lass was dancing on air the

Part Four: Tales From A Self-Published Author

You can do it!

Alan Hanna's Dublin Bookshop

entire day, above all because the old homeland showed genuine interest in my written work. Evelyn mentioned a bookshop called "Alan Hanna's" in Dublin 6 who would be processing the order for DCL. There would be no need for shipment as I was soon heading to Ireland in mid-January to attend my sister Kay's 60th birthday party. Was that great timing or what or maybe 'twas just the "Luck of the Irish"? Setting the bar high, I realized that if you want something to happen, then take a chance to pursue it, and you just never know what can materialize…

    Have I already told you how much I LOVE living in America? How Blessed it feels to be able to live out my childhood dream every single day. Three magical words always come to mind whenever I think about what America really means to me. The words are **DREAM, BELIEVE, ACHIEVE**. There is no other place in the entire world where all three words can evolve into a reality. Hard work, strength, integrity, humility, faith and determination are all requirements to make that success your very own. Many of my Irish ancestors had died while building America's skyscrapers (safe scaffolding out of the question during The Depression), canals, sewers, streets, railroads, coalmines etc. Most Irish women were forced to take on menial domestic jobs of maids, cooks, housekeepers and seamstresses. Generational Irish (and Italian) immigrants were among so many of the recorded first responders who tragically perished on September 11th of 2001. No matter the ethnicity or background; any soul fortunate enough to reach the shores of America is fully aware of the hopeful future yet to be accomplished.

    I cherish those three words so much; my son Ryan was gifted with a platinum-framed "Dream, Believe, Achieve" for Christmas 2017, complete with golden lettering to serve as future Inspiration. (Thanks to Amazon & Ross!)

    Ten days into the New Year of 2018, it soon came time to depart for the Irish capital. Confronted with a

Part Four: Tales From A Self-Published Author

packing dilemma of how to fly across the world with twenty-two paperback books, I put a plan in to motion. Twenty-two plus pounds of the fifty total allowed baggage weight would be taken up with books. Somehow, I made it work by stuffing stray books into carryon bags and mission impossible accomplished. You'd have thought I was sneaking contraband on to the plane instead of precious book cargo. At least that's my story and I'm sticking to it.

Upon arrival at a misty/foggy Dublin Airport in the wee hours of a freezing January morning, I slowly exhaled a breath of Celtic Pride. I couldn't help but feel that this homecoming was somehow different from all past visits. Had my parents still been living, they would have been so proud of their Adventurous daughter having left the nest thirty plus years earlier and now a published author.

Over the festive weekend for my sister's fabulous birthday celebrations, I got to share drinks with my old school friends/sisters Moira and Ann. Over the past ten months, both had happily read the contents of my memoir. Moira acknowledged that she now knew the full story on exactly where I had gone since leaving home a year after high school. Ann exclaimed "I have two words for you – Celtic Warrior" and that she had completed reading it in a week, while sick at home from work. How very kind of my dear old friends from our convent-educated days. With parting words: "There's going to be a movie someday and Saoirse Ronan will play you!" Ah, sure who knows girls, maybe one day indeed? Following their departure and not one to rest on my laurels, I began circulating book cards among the many laid back Sunday pub-goers. They were probably wondering where this super-energized entity had emerged from...Ha-ha! You know the Latin phrase: Carpe Diem/Sieze the Day. There's no time like the present. One of my favorite quotes is: "Don't put off until tomorrow what you can do today."

HOW TO PROMOTE THAT BOOK YOU WROTE

Monday, January 15th had finally arrived; the exciting day of delivering ten books to Dublin City Libraries. Setting off with my sister, umbrellas in hand with yours truly on a secret adrenaline rush, we boarded the half-full Luas train "into town" (That's how we always talked whenever heading for the center of Dublin City). The first of three stops was a book drop/gift for Clodagh at Creative Ireland in Pearse Street Public Library. Along with my sister's helpful navigation, since I had forgotten the way, (left home in 1981) we headed towards our second destination. Passing by an old familiar building brought back memories of our first temporary lodging after our summer of 1969 arrival from London. Our parents had decided to bring us home to grow up Ireland. As decades go by, familiar sights and sounds have a way of capturing those long forgotten moments of nostalgia. Time stands still for just a brief moment before distraction soon jolts you back to the reality of the present.

The second stop was proving a tad more complicated since we had to jump back on the Luas (tram), with hopes of locating Alan Hanna's bookshop in nearby Rathmines. As with any capital or large city, prepare to walk endlessly and always wear comfortable shoes. Whenever in Dublin, I am always grateful when it's not raining as walking, while wrestling with an umbrella in the wind is not a fun activity!

After what seemed like forever, we finally arrived at our destination. I felt relief at the prospect of relinquishing a heavy plastic bag filled with paperback books (my very own). Enquiring the whereabouts of my contact, Mary, I was promptly told she was still at lunch. No worries, with a small café towards the back of the quaint bookshop, we decided a spot of lunch was in order. Another half hour later (after all, I had one last stop to make), we were informed she was now at her desk eating a sandwich, after giving her dog a quick walk from her nearby home. Not wishing to be rude but still excited about this historic event (a Dublin girl, turned author living in Colorado, USA), I proudly extended the bag of books. "Just put it over there!" came an abrupt response as she was consumed with another important project and would check them over later. Like a deer in the headlights, I began to ask innocently: "Do I get paid today?" Not on your life Annie; did you really think it was going to be so straight forward? To cut a long story short, I did get paid a few months later after a crash course on how to create a PayPal invoice, account etc. And let's not even get started on the frustrating international bank transfer affair as that just might make for an entire book chapter on patience and tolerance.

Well alrighty then; it was now time for the third and final stop at yet another smaller, also quaint little book shop just across the River Liffey by way of the Ha'penny Bridge. A bit of history: The Ha'penny Bridge is located near O'Connell Street and Temple Bar and crosses the River Liffey. Constructed from iron in 1816, costing three thousand pounds, it acted as a toll bridge, charging people a ha'penny or a half penny to cross.

I had called the Winding Stair manager a month earlier, offering to drop off a complimentary book copy (among the twenty-two in my bags) for her perusal. She greeted me, as much as one can without my being of much significance, i.e. a famous author. Might she consider an extra copy to perhaps place on the shelves? "Oh no thanks!" came her quick reply, while tossing (oops, I meant placing) it to one side.

During an all too brief visit, I had touched on how much fun it might be to someday make a small guest appearance on "The Late Late Show". This is a Friday night variety show that has aired on Irish television since the mid-1960s, making it the second oldest of its kind in the world. To further shatter such a frail ego, I was consequently advised upon that it would probably never happen since the show centered more on celebrity-written books and not unknown authors (like yours truly). There went a shattered dream. Maybe not so much as returning home, I did lots of detective work and found the right producers to contact. Although polite messages fluctuated back and forth, the allotted Friday night has still not been set in stone.... As of yet!

A gentle Irish rain (or typical Irish depressing drizzle) had begun to fall as we crossed the bridge once again to catch our bus home on the opposite side of the Liffey River. Waiting in the long queue (line), we finally managed to snag two downstairs seats on the second bus that came. Buses during the rush hour often arrive jam packed full of weary commuters returning home after a long work day. With words of negativity still echoing in my ears, I reflected: "Nobody in the world has a clue about all the Life Dreams I have already made come true, nor the ton of Adventures that brought me back here!" One thing I would never do is to try and shatter another's dream, whatever it may be.

Upon approaching our final stop, (yes, it was still raining) we gathered up our bags and umbrellas and headed towards the front exit. Halfway there, some commuters were descending the stairs of the double-decker bus and out of habit, I let a few go ahead. As the last young lady reached the bottom step, I nodded for her to proceed. Warmly clad in a black bomber jacket, she smiled while muttering a word of gratitude. It was just at the exact moment having stepped in front of me that I caught sight of the white lettering on the back of her jacket. Those special three words of "**Dream, Believe, Achieve**" came into sight, serving as a gentle reminder to "Never Give Up" on all of our individual Dreams, come what may...

"When you are old and grey and full of sleep and nodding by the fire, take down this book, and slowly read, and dream of the soft look your eyes had once, and of their shadows deep."
                              -William Butler Yeats "When You are Old"

Part Four: Tales From A Self-Published Author
Chapter 4: Getting to Know Colorful Colorado

"The words ran away from me."
– Edna O'Brien/Country Girl

Upon returning to the sunny blue skies of Colorado, my mind was firmly set upon yet another New Year venture of book-promotions. On snowy January afternoons, I soon began compiling a long list of all the public libraries across the State of Colorado. Thanks to PPLD, Celtic Road Home had already been placed on local library book shelves. However, this Dublin gal had her sights on the wild blue yonder and faraway destinations.

Gathering together the scribbled notes, I began calling around six libraries a day as promoting yourself (gift of the Celtic gab on my part) can quickly become an exhausting process. The initial approach was quickly modified from my original greeting opener: "Hi, How are you today?" (Not another telemarketer) to: "May I please speak to your library director?" As luck would have it, not only did the recipient enjoy listening to a soft, Irish lilt but also fully supported local authors. What a wonderful way to introduce a new book, while remembering, you still have to sell yourself/your new book even on the best of days. Each and every phone call/email will slowly contribute towards a flow of recognition as a new author. Fun times are ahead.

Take advantage of the unexpected geography lesson as you discover your neighboring towns and cities where you live. Starting with the distance in miles, nearby towns, connecting library districts, seasonal

Nearly Missed Holyoke Street Sign

Highlands Ranch Library, CO

Part Four: Tales From A Self-Published Author

harvests, famous landmarks etc., it feels like a new expeditionary venture. Albeit from a safe, faceless distance.

Although larger library districts often maintain an established protocol for new author acquisitions, I felt much more of a kindred spirit connecting with the tiny, rural community branches. The essence of close-knit get-togethers throughout the year often revolves around the provincial library. Not only is it a thrill for them to host a local author but also attracts those long-forgotten readers and helps add to their annual appropriated library budget. In fact, there was even one tiny library (Fowler, CO) that occupied an allocated room/library in the town courthouse. A few days later, I mailed them a complimentary book to add to their collection.

The following encounters are a sampling of author talks/events (2017-19) that took place across the beautiful Centennial state of Colorado, the 38th state admitted to the Union in 1876. While each library visit was unique, the heartfelt welcomes, inquisitive faces and encouragement remained consistent throughout.

Colorado Springs, CO

The second-largest city (after Denver) is home to the United States Air Force Academy, Garden of the Gods, US Olympic Training Center, Pikes Peak/Cog Railway, The Broadmoor Hotel/Resort and so much more... What a Blessing to have lived here for nearly three decades. The stunning view of Pikes Peak (14,115 ft) paired against a daily azure blue sky resembles nothing short of a dream-filled landscape.

Pikes Peak Library District had been kind enough to have invited me back for three consecutive years to participate in "Mountain of Authors". What an honor to be included among such celebrated, fellow local authors.

Penrose, East and Old Colorado City Libraries etc. played a part in local author events throughout the first two years. Unfortunately, the latter two are still on the books due to a spring snowstorm and a summer hailstorm....that's Mother Nature for you. But wait, we haven't even hit The Plandemic yet...!

Westcliffe, CO

Tucked away at the base of the Sangre de Cristo (blood of Christ) Mountains to the west and the Wet Mountains to the east, Westcliffe is a picturesque little town of about six hundred inhabitants. If you were to ask; they would most likely wish to keep it that way too. During the peak of snowy winter months, the town is often isolated for days at a time, making it an idyllic location for those desiring a quiet quality of life.

Cathy McCarthy, the director had kindly invited me to visit on the Friday of the upcoming Memorial Day weekend, typically the first weekend of summer. After a ninety-minute scenic drive along desolate country roads, we stumbled upon a picture-postcard main street with a backdrop of magnificent mountain views.

Contently snagging a parking space upfront, we entered the West Custer library, arms laden down with book supplies. All was quiet within, except for a solitary English lady speaking with a heavy Geordie (?) accent. Annie here would soon require some adjustments on becoming acquainted with the sloooower way of life in these here mountain towns... A smiling Cathy momentarily came bustling in, thoughtfully pointing to a flyer on the front door about the Celtic visit. Having the name of Cathy McCarthy meant there was a lot of Irish heritage on her husband's side. Originally from the east coast, followed by a short stint in Denver; the town of Westcliffe was to become her Dream & Forever Paradise.

As was to be expected; with the beautiful weather outside and summer on the horizon, we were unlucky with having an audience. Not to worry; it had resulted in a lovely day out to a new unknown location on our bucket list. Thanks Cathy for your gracious hospitality and for being the first out of town historic library visit for Celtic Road Home: A Memoir.

Idaho Springs, CO

Gold was first discovered in this mining town back in 1859. Several mining tours provide insight into the history of this little town along the I-70 corridor heading towards well-known ski towns like Aspen and Vail. Most of the historic buildings here have been well-preserved including the library, Tommyknocker Brewery and Beau Jo's Colorado Style Pizza.

The Idaho Springs Library Book Club sat in attendance while I happily briefed them on the overall book's storyline. Most of the ladies had already read or were still reading; dutifully holding hardback copies in their hands. That was a pleasant sight to behold as I quickly discovered local library districts shared book copies from each town. There was much animated back and forth as well as the reading aloud of several favorite book excerpts. The second mountain town to be discovered via recently self-published author, Annie The Explorer: Check.

Sterling, CO

This three-day trip was part of a multiple library visit in mid-August of 2019 to include nearby Fleming, Holyoke and Fort Morgan. The largest city in the northeastern part of the state; Sterling is a farm and ranch community with deep held roots on the Colorado prairie. The very first pioneers in the area came by way of the Overland Trail, one that takes you back in time while touring the local museum of the same name.

Following a hotel check-in (handicap accessible room mix-up/last room available, makes you feel so fortunate for good health), we headed for a quick bite at the nearby Village Inn. Missy, our super-friendly server (also cook) was a recovering addict who now loved taking photos of thunder and lightning storms. I'll bet those were some amazing images while also dangerous at the best of times. Upon discovering the reason for our stay in Sterling, she began to react in excitement, announcing: "Hey, we have an author in the house! I read about you in the local paper and couldn't get the evening off to come and see you talk. I just know you're gonna be famous someday!" As my dear old Mum used to say: "Well, that just beats the band!" What more of a welcome could I have anticipated? Small town friendliness cannot be beat, no matter where in the world you happen to find yourself. Relax and enjoy the slower and thoughtful way of life. Guess that makes me a city girl at heart then…

The setting of Sterling Library was flanked with two sides of protection, a police and fire station; I guess the safest place to be, right? Beautiful inside, Kathy the long-term director soon greeted us, stating she had lived there for most of her life. Ten locals sat comfortably nearby as our evening soon began. One gentleman had driven in especially from the farming area, stating how he would be starting travels to faraway places following long working years on the farmlands. Another older couple spoke of having driven all around Ireland a decade before.

On our return to the hotel, we got lost in the dark with all the summertime road construction. While getting out of the car outside our hotel, I began to hear an unusual sound in the air and asked Jimmie. Turned out to be locusts, but what was most unusual was how the soft buzzing would radiate from tree to tree. One tree would begin buzzing as another went completely silent. Ok, it was now time for rest with a new exciting day of upcoming library stops the very next day in Fleming and Higgenbotham.

Part Four: Tales From A Self-Published Author

Fleming, CO

Sterling Correctional Facility (Prison) was to our right as we exited Sterling on the twelve-mile drive towards Fleming. I felt sorry for all those incarcerated on the other side on such a hot 100-degree summer's day and wished them some positive energy.

Fleming is a tiny one-street town with Bully's, the local bar/dining haunt amidst grain silos where farmers stored grain, wheat etc, until ready to be sold to market. I finally learned the purpose of those metal buildings, thanks to the Mississippi cotton-picking childhood of my wonderful husband.

Fleming School was the second library stop and the notice on the locked door "Armed Security on site" somehow created a feeling of safety as we were buzzed inside. Sandy warmly greeted us and showed us around her school library setting. Not only the librarian, she held multiple job descriptions as it became abundantly clear of her Love and Devotion to all the school kids there. Also a young and vibrant grandmother, she took pride in each and every child in her care.

During the following two hours, we greeted/chatted with teenagers (two girls with stars in their eyes upon hearing of places I had lived like London, Paris, Madrid etc.), a recently-retired teacher with pension issues, a Welsh computer whizz who would love to read my book as well as a few other visitors.

Upon leaving, Sandy kindly gifted me with a $50 check for having taken the time and effort to come and visit their school. She also included a crocheted dish towel she had just finished moments before as well as a jar of homemade jalapeno/raspberry jelly. I just adore the warmth and hospitality of small town America. The return invitation may take some time but will most definitely be considered in future years.

Holyoke, CO

After breakfast the following morning, I received another library invitation from another Sandy, this time from Vail. Would I be interested in a late October date to come and speak there? How much was my fee? After mentioning how an offer of payment fluctuated @ $100, the issue was soon settled upon. Ooh, stunning Vail Mountain in the snow; I could hardly wait.

Prior to our departure to Holyoke, I had made a hair appointment for a quick wash and blow dry behind a strip mall in Sterling. On a tight time constraint (my bad), I began to get antsy after the 3pm time was inching towards three-thirty. Remember Annie, small town and the slower pace of living. Yadda, yadda, yadda... attempting to teach an old dog new tricks is much easier said than done, lol! By the time we rushed towards the exit, yours truly with slightly damp hair, all while avoiding high speed along construction roads; we somehow made it to Holyoke with mere minutes to spare.

Missing our first right turn, we quickly took the next one and right as we rounded the corner, my husband noticed a large wooden sign on the opposite corner. It turned out to be a sandwich board advertising my book event, offering hot tea and scones. Had we taken that first turn, we would never have seen it. Isn't Life funny sometimes and how each and every choice we make always has a reason, consequence etc?

Hastily crossing the quiet residential street, we were greeted by the appearance of a black cat. Was that the gift of a positive omen? Heginbotham library (actually a house) was celebrating its centennial since construction in 1919 and is also listed on the National Register of Historic Places. It reminded me of a fairy tale building complete with ornate and delicate details, with low walls amid a garden blooming with colorful flowers.

I felt slightly hesitant upon entering based on alarming details the "running late" hair lady had recounted back in Sterling. Growing up in Holyoke, she recounted an alleged story of back in the day before Mr. William Higgenbotham (the owner) had donated his house to the library following his death. Apparently he had been a former KKK leader in the area. She also referred to a local law still on the books about non-white visitors to the town. Well, well, well; with my hubby being Black-American, would I have something to say about that, being an expressive Irish lady and all!

Entering along a dimly-lit hallway, we were greeted by a smiling director called Kathy along with her assistant Lisa. Noticing the large black and white framed portrait behind the desk, I politely asked if that was Mr. Heginbotham and indeed it was. "Now listen, William; I want you to know we are now living in 2019, so you had better not mess up our evening by way of flickering lights, etc. Is that clear?" Lisa just quietly giggled as she led us to a cosy space of the library where I could comfortably set up.

For the next few hours, we enjoyed hot tea, scones and banter about all things Irish and on taking chances in Life. Kathy's brother and sister in-law had just moved into a former mortuary which they were converting into a house. That was something never heard of before with of course, the question soon posed: "Is it haunted?" Silly, of course it was. Ooh, the stories they began to tell... As we all departed into the evening darkness, the group stated they had not had such a fun evening in a long time. Glad to be of Celtic service and to answer your question: No, the lights never flickered, not even once.

Fort Morgan, CO

Fort Morgan, also part of the Overland Trail is best known as the high-school hometown of the famous musician Glenn Miller (Big Band era of the 1930s and 1940s) who was awarded the first gold record in history. In 1920, while playing for his high school Marooner's football team, he was named the best left-end in Colorado. What a talented guy. The Fort Morgan Museum is also home to the Glenn Miller Theatre exhibit where you can hear his music, while admiring photographs and other lifetime memorabilia.

"Save the Best for last" as the old saying goes and that is exactly what comes to mind with the Fort Morgan Library, culminating into our fourth and final stop. Despite the strange musky odor that sneaks into the air (due to the nearby Western Sugar Co-Op location) and ominous dark clouds overhead, we opened up the doors to an exquisite library. At the entrance, glancing at your profile poster on the door window doesn't harm the nerves either. Constructed in 1880, the library doubled its space in 1915 to become the beautiful building that stands today.

The elegance of the entryway (both outside and inside) was tastefully complemented by the talented sculptures of a local artist by the name of Luann Anderson. This amazing creator had sadly passed away a few years earlier from cancer. What a magical combination of statues depicting a woman holding hands with young, playful children. For some reason, it reminded me of the Great Hunger/Famine years of Ireland's history and the emigration of so much Irish ancestry around the globe. Makes me sad, even just thinking about it.

Setting up in an open area adjacent to a large window, I began to distribute flyers while asking if anyone in the audience had ever been to Ireland. A few retold stories of their vacations there as we giggled on the cultural differences etc. Once the seats were occupied, I headed towards the podium that had been kindly set up in advance. At precisely the moment that I began to read, a huge ray of sunlight began to lighten up the entire area, blinding some of the people sitting in that spot, including a little girl. Uncomfortable, she wanted to move with her mother insisting she just stay still. Sorry, little one. Wow, what truly felt like a Divine moment was later justified by Lanny; the Library Director of Programs admitting the library elf had indeed acknowledged our enchanted evening. What an honor to have been selected among the first of five authors in their "2019 Fall into Winter Colorado Author Series".

The other miracle of that magical evening transpired when for the first time of twenty-six years living in the United States, I finally met another Doolan! Her name was Sarah Doolan and there's even a photo to prove it. On the drive back to the hotel in Sterling, a Shuffle Josh Groban song began to play called "Alla luce del sole" (By the light of the sun)....it was then I knew it had been my Sweet Mum who had stopped by to bestow her Blessings of Love via a bursting of sunlight...Love and Miss you each and every day. As a final bonus of three, a Shamrock Foods truck had also directly driven right past our café window a few days before in Fort Morgan, so Dad was also connected with the magic of Fort Morgan. We will return someday soon for sure to that special place.

Highlands Ranch, CO

On a warm spring Saturday, courtesy of Deb at Douglas County Libraries, we pulled up to a newly-renovated building in the upscale community south of Denver. In a rush, due to traffic on I-25 (what's new), we were ushered to one of the last unoccupied tables with the presentation just about to start. On either side were two very interesting ladies and friends. Hillary hailed from Wexford, Ireland (also married to an Air Force man) was finishing up on a children's book, while her friend was promoting her new book about Beatles songs.

There were to be twelve speakers in all with each of us allotted a five-minute slot. Luckily, I was eleventh (my lucky number) and although the crowd seemed a tad weary by then; I hopefully managed to create a little spark. I spoke of writing a tale of Celtic travels and how Maureen O'Hara's memoir called "'Tis Herself" had inspired my writing method in the second person/inviting the reader to become part of the story. A couple of funny travel tidbits and poof….the five minute buzzer sounded to announce "Time's Up!"

Some of the authors had incredible stories to tell; from a lady who had worked as a Hollywood producer alongside a famous comedian, an author/cartoonist, a lady who had lost her husband and spoke of overcoming grief and finally, an abuse Survivor. What an interesting, yet rewarding afternoon it had turned out to be. Deb, who had been battling the flu, mentioned that all books from the invited speakers would now be ordered for their library. I ordered her to go home and get some well-deserved rest, Bless her.

Florence, CO

Oil was first discovered here back in 1862, making it the first oil center west of The Mississippi River. Florence was originally built as a train depot/transportation center to haul coal from the nearby towns of Rockvale and Coal Creek. Main Street, Florence had also recently played a major part as the movie set in "Our Souls at Night" (2017) with acting veterans Robert Redford and Jane Fonda. One of the library ladies had even proudly sneaked a photo with Mr. Redford during a film break, stating he was the perfect gentleman. To check out a young and handsome Mr. Redford, watch the 1973 movie "The Way We Were" with Barbara Streisand; among one of my favorites. Have the Kleenex ready at some point too….

Vicki, our gracious host, commented on how she had just finished reading "Celtic Road Home" the night before and was feeling INSPIRED to complete whatever current goals she needed to get done. What moving feedback…

All was quiet for a while until a regular patron stopped by. Negative by nature, (Vicki's words) he inquisitively pulled up a chair and chatted for a while, mostly about his disgust with current political affairs and so on. As he finally rose to leave, I posed the question: "Imagine what a wonderful world it would be if we could all just agree to disagree?" Vicki later stated: "That's one of our most disgruntled library members and you handled him beautifully!". Calling it a day, we lazily strolled across the street to enjoy an early dinner at the Chinese restaurant before heading back to the Springs.

Lamar, CO

Lamar is located in the heart of Colorado with two major US Highway connections north to south from Canada to Mexico and from the east to west coast. It is also a renowned birding site with over four hundred bird species such as red-bellied woodpeckers. For visitors arriving from the east, it becomes the first stop in the Rocky Mountain state and sits at the furthest south-eastern tip of Prowers County.

The three-hour scenic drive took us through Pueblo, Rocky Ford (famous for melons) Las Animas, a stinky town called Swink (cattle stockyard) and La Junta etc.

The Lamar Public Library (1906) is built with an impressive interior, complete with connecting sun-filled hallways. Arriving about ten minutes late, (getting lost just before Lamar) we were hastily escorted to a large room with a waiting audience of about twenty-five. With no time to set-up, I apologized profusely while beginning my presentation as my hubby/partner in crime managed to quietly assemble book materials behind me. How would I ever manage without his amazing help?

Book-signing can consist of both a fun but exhausting experience that is often frustrating; be it an individual cash sale or fighting with your smart phone for complicated (for me at the time) transactions. At least, I speak rhetorically for those of us Baby-Boomers. Before long, it was all over and not one to count my earnings (I choose not to make book/events about money, while recognizing the importance of income/expenses). I somehow managed to misplace a $20 bill while talking with a local man who had mentioned he would buy the book with his upcoming Social Security check. Bless him.

All was not lost however; I still managed to recuperate half at a gas-station in Las Animas (famous for being part of the historic Santa Fe Trail) where a young clerk bought a copy for $10. Never having left the area, she hoped to one day pluck up the courage to explore parts unknown of our big, wide world. I sincerely hope she someday gets to honor her wish…

Montrose, CO

The south-western area of Montrose is steeped in history, having once been home to the original Ute Indians who were later relocated to the nearby state of Utah. Originally, with names like Pomona, Dad's Town and Uncompahghre, the small city finally became known as Montrose based on a character in a Walter Scott novel "The Legend of Montrose". It was originally intended as a main supplier to nearby mining communities but eventually developed into a farming economy.

Today, it remains a popular vacation spot with tons of options for hiking, biking, rafting, rock-climbing, including its proximity to nearby Ouray, Black Canyon, Uncompahghre National Forest, Gunnison Gorge Wilderness Area etc. The scenic ski town of Telluride beckons a short ninety-minute drive away.

Following a brief stint at "Maggie's Book Store", we dined early at a local pizza place and headed to the Montrose Public Library. This time, there appeared a quick video advert on the screen in the entry way on my author visit. Wow, that was a nice touch and ultra modern to put it mildly. I wish I could have bottled up

Part Four: Tales From A Self-Published Author

each and every library event as they were all so unique. You can always do like I did and keep a little diary as you go.

Taylor helped to set up chairs (many of which would not be needed) in a modernly-spaced room. The evening passed quickly as with any small audience; the author talk soon transformed into chats on travel to Ireland etc. With the dark October evening, beckoning the long drive back to our lodging in nearby Norwood that holds a treacherous cliffhanging drive on its approach to the tiny town. Grateful for not having to drive along its precipice, (thanks to my wonderful driver/hubby) it was still a scary experience and one we had to take a total of four times. You bet I counted each and every to and fro too…

Incidentally, as you leave Montrose, before reaching Ridgway (the halfway mark on the 90 minute drive to Norwood), look out for a little open area on your left called Dennis Weaver Park. It is aptly named after the 1970s actor who starred in "McCloud" and "Gunsmoke" to name just a few. A tidbit for those among you old enough to remember those TV shows. Mr. Weaver had opted to live in nearby Ridgway after his three sons Rick, Rusty and Robby, regular skiers in nearby Telluride, proposed he buy land there and grow his own food. He indeed became a permanent resident in 1990, donating sixty acres to the town of Ridgway which were converted into a public park a year after his February, 2006 death.

Following short daytime visits to Norwood and the nearby stunning mountain town of Telluride, it soon came time to head home again. Although it was only early October, a snowstorm was heading in our direction (sounds like a Hallmark Christmas movie!) which made for a slick and icy drive through Monarch Pass. Upon arrival home into a warm garage, blocks of ice broke off while opening the car door; that's just how cold the weather had suddenly changed. One moment, a stunning landscape of color-changing aspens lay before us on meandering mountain ways only to change within hours to white snowy skies above. That's Colorado for you; with the chance of experiencing four seasons in one single day. Sadly, our sweet twenty-year old Calico cat Maya, had awaited our home-coming only to spend one final day with us before peacefully passing away in her sleep a day later. We will see you on the other side one day Sweet Girl...

Vail, CO

If you have never been; you must surely add this picturesque slice of Heaven to your travel/bucket list. I promise you will never live to regret it. Nestled along the I-70 corridor (an hour and forty-minute drive from nearby Denver), it lies at the base of Vail Mountain and is home to the massive Vail Ski Resort. Open year round, it also hosts golfing, hiking, summer activities and festivals. I enjoy it best in winter though, as it resembles a snowy village in the Swiss Alps and remains by far, my favorite of all the ski towns in Colorado. Not exactly cheap, you can always find residence just outside of Vail, while still savoring the exquisite details of its quaintness and beauty. Strolling about or jumping on the complimentary shuttle bus, you will feel like you're in a village in Switzerland with photo ops to fill your heart's desire.

Luckily, Jimmie had advised us to store snow boots in the car and oh boy, was I glad he did as it turned out to be a freezing, cold afternoon in late October. Vail sits at an altitude of 8,150 feet above sea level (Colorado Springs is at 6,035 while Denver, called the Mile High City stands at exactly one mile above sea level at 5.280) which means your ears will definitely pop as you drive towards its higher elevation.

To date, it is the most beautiful library I have ever had the pleasure to visit. Built into the side of a hill, the picture-postcard ambience of its interior will entice you to never leave, (unlike the song Hotel California). But wait until you relax by the welcoming fireplace, softly gazing upon the snowy evergreens along the hillside.

Part Four: Tales From A Self-Published Author

Pure Heaven is the only description that comes to mind. Regardless of the impending author talk; I didn't want to leave that cozy part of the library one bit. But as always, needs must, right?

At the appropriate time, (and not a moment earlier) I was led to another long room on the other side of the library with large photograph-framed adorned walls. A famous National Geographic photographer by the name of Jim Richardson had just recently hosted a talk, kindly permitting his pictures to stay a little longer. What a moving exhibit called "Women Farmers" of painstakingly captured natural images of female breadwinners from all corners of the globe. What incredible and artistic talent. It was also the very last day before they were to be taken down and returned to their rightful owner, making it feel like such an honor.

Due to the inclement weather, I really didn't expect a high turnout. However, the less than a dozen kind souls who did manage to attend certainly received many thanks on our part. We were eternally grateful for the warm drinks, snacks and books signed before making the snowy and icy commute safely back home once again.

"Life isn't about finding yourself. Life is about creating yourself"
–George Bernard Shaw

Part Four: Tales From A Self-Published Author
Chapter 4: Onwards and Upwards

"Vision is the art of seeing what is invisible to others."
                                                    –Jonathan Swift

2017 through 2019, I poured my heart and soul into each and every book invitation, be it a talk/signing, collaborated event, podcast, book club, meet and greet; you name it, the Honor was all mine. Should an author ever reach the moment of reflection with: "Is that it?" That will all depend on who you happen to ask and in what timeframe the question is posed.

For me personally, I still have so much more ground to cover in sharing such INSPIRATIONAL messages to help guide readers towards achieving their Life goals, while never giving up in the interim.

Throughout most of 2019, I never stopped emailing libraries all around the United States and the world. Thousands of messages sent back and forth became a daily habit, never knowing what unexpected response lay in wait upon the light of each new dawn. This little girl inside became magically transported to faraway gems like Tasmania, South Africa, Fiji, Hong Kong, Brazil and too many others to mention. The cultures of the world had secretly opened as both enlightening and inviting at the same time.

IngramSpark is a wonderful introduction for your book placement in more than 40,000 bookstores and libraries across the world. In the summer of 2018, I also uploaded my eBook to Draft2Digital whose online platform distributes to Overdrive, Baker & Taylor,

Part Four: Tales From A Self-Published Author

Barnes & Noble At Last!

Tattered Cover Denver

BorrowBooks and many other worldwide booksellers. It was so very exciting to discover all the places across the world that now offered my book on display.

One of the most challenging times happened while uploading book details etc. with Nielsen Title Editor based in the UK. For my un-techie mind, the nitty gritty details proved so cumbersome at times prompting a few overseas, early morning calls. It took more than two dozen emails back and forth, and honestly, I really considered abandoning the entire process. Looking at the bigger picture however inspired me forwards to get it done. Those stubborn creases got finally ironed out, proving never giving up will always get you through it all somehow.

Nielsen Book Data now had Celtic Road Home in their system which meant UK book distributors like Bertrams and Gardeners now had sales access to libraries and bookstores. In addition, WH Smith, Waterstones, Book Depository, Better World Books, Blackwells, Awesome Books, Foyles, etc. also carried the paperback/hardback and eBook versions online. What a treat.

Researching email addresses of all the libraries across the UK as well as in my native Ireland enabled hundreds of promotional messages/responses. On several early mornings, you'd find me in the kitchen (so as not to awake the household) calling libraries in Wales, Oxfordshire (and many other shires...), Scotland etc. to establish the correct contact. The experiment didn't last long however not only due to the early rising (seven hours behind) but also the long distance phone calls. Numerous libraries on that side of the pond now carry the book; couldn't tell you exactly where...which makes it even more special, wouldn't you agree?

Oh gosh; what else did Annie get up to over the past few years with her Celtic memoir? Let's see now. It feels like a decade has passed by since that early March of 2017.

Part Four: Tales From A Self-Published Author

Upon discovery of writing.ie (an Irish website for authors), I was invited to compose a thousand-word blog on the challenges and rewards of writing a self-published book. In turn, they not only published it but posted a book link. That was most kind and felt like another hometown reward of sorts.

In September of 2018, my family and two close girlfriends set off on a trip to Dublin (the girls' very first time in Ireland) to celebrate special birthdays. A couple months before, I had been in communications with the editor of "Woman's Weekly" about CRH. Always kind, Aine would try to add a book mention in a summer/early fall issue. One of her last messages affirmed it would be included in an upcoming September edition.

On September 11th, after checking in early to our hotel near the main thoroughfare of O'Connell St., we ventured out for some breakfast. Passing a newsagent's (convenience store) I stepped inside to search for the latest issue of "Woman's Way" (delivered hours earlier), nervously searched inside and…..there it was! What a Glorious "Welcome Home to Dublin" and early Birthday gift to boot.

It goes to show that if you believe strongly enough in the conviction of your book/story and never give up, nobody else will either.

Back in Boulder, CO, there was another Irish lady from KGNU (a community radio station in Boulder) who had invited me on her podcast. We chatted about CRH, our own Celtic background, adjustments to living in America and beyond. It was the second podcast following an earlier one at the Heritage Center in magical Manitou Springs with an adorable couple (Erick & Tammila Wright) who also happen to be formidable ghost-hunters in the local area.

The most recent podcast took place at Right Time Radio in Canyon City. A charming town that hosts white river rafting along The Arkansas River, as well as The

Royal Gorge Bridge, Park, railway, Holy Cross Abbey/ Winery, etc.

Up early with the birds and luckily having no snow to compete with, we began the sunrise drive. Heading towards the majestic mountains near Fort Carson (army base) along pretty winding roads towards Penrose (apple farms) and finally on to Highway 50 in Canyon City.

Upon arrival at our destination, Lynn and Tom kindly escorted us into their basement studios. I might also add that both of our hosts are also exceptional writers in their own right with several books available online. Lynn Donovan writes amazing historical and temporary Romance (more than 70 on Amazon) while Tom Bruno dabbles in Sci-Fi/Speculative Fiction, Fantasy.

What amusement we had for the next couple hours, both prior and during our one-hour radio interview that went out live to the local community. First of all, neither Tom nor I had glasses to be able to decipher my book's small print. Thankfully, Lynn came to the rescue, donating her reading glasses for Tom to read the introduction of the Milan chapter. I guess you might say we were like the blind leading the blind (no pun intended) up until that moment. A classical, comical Abbott and Costello episode comes to mind...ha-ha!

Phew; what an exhilarating hour spent together, mindful of our ultra-savvy producer, Kari Jacobs who would motion us with hand signals whenever it came time for a commercial break. It really opened our eyes as to all the details behind the scenes operations of a radio station. On a final note; Write Time Radio broadcasts most Fridays from 10am to 11am on KRLN, AKA Royal Gorge Broadcasting LLC. The show both introduces and celebrates all local authors in the area. Thanks again Friends.

Tattered Cover in Denver also invited me on two separate occasions for a book event at their beautiful downtown Denver locations. The entire staff shows such

Part Four: Tales From A Self-Published Author

admiration and dedication to the art of books with the atmosphere in each individual store both magical and inviting.

A few local book clubs chose CRH (Celtic Road Home) as their book of the month choice. One in particular will always touch my heart strings forever. Ellie, a sweet lady hosted lunch for twelve plus ladies on a sweltering July afternoon out of her beautiful home. She even took the trouble of preparing bangers (sausages) and mash, a tricolor salad (colors of the Irish flag; green, white and orange) along with two Sherry Trifles for dessert. That recipe, along with Irish Coffee can both be found at the back of the CRH book. The dedicated hours taken to create such an event are truly appreciated. Thank you Ellie.

The kindness of human beings never ceases to amaze, especially when it comes from the heart.

The first two weeks of December 2019 brought about a series of three separate book invitations. An amazingly-talented artist called Mary Shell invited us to join her for early dinner before an evening at her lovely art studio along Main Street, Canyon City. In her early artsy days, she had designed the black and white newspaper stills/adverts for the famous English 1960s model Twiggy. Wow! While she rapidly painted (in between raving about CRH to her audience) we would all guess what her picture would be; often not knowing until the last moment. She painted a total of three canvases with the winners chosen via a drawing. What a positive, gutsy lady and a total pleasure to spend a chilly December evening with. Any art student fortunate enough to take one of her classes will forever be Inspired.

Many thanks to Liz Groothof Croddy; the second event included an invitation to speak at an annual end of year dinner for a local chapter of Zonta. Since 1923, this international charity has donated more than $11 million to projects benefiting more than two million women around the world. Operating locally since 1949, some of their primary objectives involve the further progress of equality for women, combating human and sex-trafficking, abuse and so much more.

The final event of the year took place at Hooked on Books in downtown Colorado Springs with the lovely Mary Ciletti and her husband Jim.

More than thirty books had been sold during the course of those three events which was a record; although the camaraderie, stimulating conversation and overall fun meant so much more.

In early 2020, in addition to public libraries, academic libraries suddenly entered the radar of even further outreach. In alphabetical order, I had reached the letter D with a few encouraging responses; a private college outside San Francisco would love for me to host their students if I was ever in the area. Another Catholic university in Indiana chuckled that I reminded them of their founder, a feisty Irish nun (also from Dublin) who never gave up either on her soul mission.

One of the upcoming classes at nearby Pikes Peak Community College was called "Celtic Mythology" on past/present Celtic authors. The Literature professor had invited me to come visit the class at some point but unfortunately, it was early March of 2020 and just before our world came to a crashing halt.

Ever since calling Stephanie at the Gazette a few years before, (that instigated a magical gateway) I had always harbored a secret wish for a book-signing at the prestigious Barnes and Noble bookstore. Currently, there are two locations in Colorado Springs and feeling adventurous, I contacted both of them. The energy/circumstances on the first call didn't pan out however, upon the second phone call; the opportunity soon arose with some Celtic convincing on my part. To help celebrate the upcoming St. Patrick's Day, wouldn't a mid-March date be ideal?

Part Four: Tales From A Self-Published Author

Unfortunately, Sunday, March 15th coincided with the beginning of the world lockdown. Sitting at a designated table in a lovely but empty bookstore, the few customers rushing by were wary of even touching, never mind buying a physical book. Nevertheless, I will always treasure the fact that I did actually make it to Barnes & Noble (one of my dreams) after all and still have the treasured store banner as a memory. Perhaps they will invite me back one day….

Since early January, I had been following a YouTube channel detailing what was on the horizon, holding out Hope it wouldn't become a big deal. On the contrary, nobody could have ever predicted how this has changed our world forevermore. We must diligently learn to adapt while moving **Onwards and Upwards** and above all, always live without fear.

"I'm gonna make the rest of my life the best of my life."
–Matt Hogan

Part Four: Tales from a Self-Published Author
Chapter 6: Reflections: What I have Learned

"Life is a journey that must be traveled no matter how bad the roads and accommodations."
–Oliver Goldsmith

Having lived half of my life in Europe and almost another half in America has gifted me with Life Experiences and Wisdom beyond mere words could ever describe. Never would I have dared contemplate that not only one but two books would play a significant role along my journey. Who knows what possibilities lie in wait for anyone of us? It certainly just takes that one initial thought or idea to create the spark that motivates the voyage to wherever you want to go. Every decision you make really all does depend on you.

The extraordinary lessons I have learned from plucking up the courage to write, self-publish and promote my very first book has taught me so much more about humanity than I could have ever envisioned. Included are kindness, competitiveness, envy, grace, ego, gratitude, enlightenment and so much more. Besides the kindness of strangers, one of the biggest learning curves came from words of promise that actually never came to fruition. Always observe what people say and whether they walk the walk or just talk the talk. Does that make sense? If you strive to do all the work necessary to promote the book all by yourself, it will always be due to your own timeless efforts.

In darker moments, whenever a feeling of not-being-good-enough sneaks in, I take a peek at the nine

Part Four: Tales From A Self-Published Author

Vail Library, CO

Dad Saying "Hello"

plus pages on Google and all the crazy, hard work shows. So yes, you will always be good enough when you put your heart and soul into any Life effort you are willing to undertake.

Here are some thought-provoking reasons/outcomes/testimonies as to why self-publishing a book has proved such a rewarding and worthy endeavor.

- A few weeks after gifting the four young ladies, who operated the local UPS Store, Ashley the manager shared the following story. While preparing to leave church the Sunday before, she had set her CRH copy on the pew. Suddenly, a lady tapped her on the shoulder from behind with: "I'm reading that very same book and met the author at a recent book-signing!"

- Before one of two surgeries, Gabby (Mom to two young boys) at the reception/in-patient hospital desk exclaimed:"Ann, I bought your book on Amazon and read it in three days! My hubby told me to come to bed late one night but I told him that I was unable to put it down. Your book has inspired me to go back to school and get my degree!"

- The receptionist at a nearby skin-care clinic was busy on the phone while I was checking-in for an appointment. As soon as she hung up from her call: "Ann, I LOVE your life story and feel like I'm a part of it!" It was so funny to see all the faces in the reception area look up in surprise along with a lady requesting the title and where it could be found….

- Sarah September, a budding and upcoming fantasy writer (Fort Morgan Library) read the entire book in one night (what?), felt inspired to finally finish up on her first book draft.

- Anita wants to now travel the world before Life passes her by.

- Lindsay plans to visit The Emerald Isle/Ireland

- John says to "Never be afraid to go out and chase your Dreams!"

Part Four: Tales from A Self-Published Author

- A lady from the UK mentioned how she had been knocked back many times in Life but still managed to accomplish a few goals.
- After emailing a complimentary pdf copy to a rural library in the Australian outback, came a warm reply from a sage Aborigine with the kind words of: "Thank you for your gift and God Bless you. Your country, Ireland has also suffered greatly, like our ancestors and the Irish are such lovely, kind people!"
- Tracy from Nielsen Title in London offered the following advice: "if you have a book worthy of reading, you must create an eBook version so that it can be shared with the world!"
- A beautiful and smart special-needs young man, following one of my "Inspirational" book sessions excitedly exclaimed "TED Talks" ("A non-profit devoted to spreading ideas, usually in the form of short, powerful talks.")
- Having the book compared to other writings/Irish authors in my genre
- Discovering all the libraries worldwide who now carried Celtic Road Home

What an exhilarating ride the last five years has turned out to be. As long as Life grants me breath, I shall never carry any regrets about embarking upon this literary venture. Interacting with people from all walks of life, exploring new locales, both near and far, seeing smiling and amused faces, getting lost in the middle of nowhere, meeting my first Doolan in America, uplifting and coaxing the next writer. All of those reasons and millions more can also play a part of your future should you wish to contribute to the ever-expanding reading world. So very glad I did...

"I've learned that people will forget what you said, people will forget what you did, but people will never forget how you made them feel."
-Maya Angelou

Epilogue

At this farewell stage of "How to Promote that Book you Wrote" my sincere hope is that you have uncovered a few tips and ideas to guide you along the way towards self-publishing your very own book. Perhaps one day soon, you too will get to savor all the up and down experiences from first holding a physical copy of your hard work to manifesting its importance to the world.

It will undoubtedly become a journey of a lifetime; one that you will always cherish even if your decision is to only publish your book and do nothing more. Perhaps it will become a befitting family keepsake, lasting many generations to come.

Whatever future your book may hold, you must always allow your intuition to take the lead, heading in the direction that is most advantageous to your everyday life. If you do this; I promise you many moments of fulfillment and accomplishment. Dedicating time and energy to your written work will in time provide all kinds of feedback. Just remember to never take others' words to heart for only you have put your heart and soul into your story.

Reviews will come in time, if they're meant to be. It's easier said than done to believe they really don't matter but in this world of likes/dislikes, it doesn't hurt either. As far as I'm concerned, you can never have too many book reviews.Thank you so very much for taking your precious time in reading How To Promote that Book you Wrote. It means the world and without further ado, from my heart to yours, please accept these departing words from a favorite Irish Blessing:

May the road rise to meet you
May the wind be always at your back
May the sun shine warm upon your face;
The rains fall soft upon your fields
And until we meet again
May God hold you in the palm of his hand

God Bless, Good Luck and May you have more good days ahead... Slainte! Ann

About the Author:

Ann Doolan-Fox is a proud U.S. citizen (1998), originally from Dublin, Ireland. For twelve years in her younger days, she lived all over Europe, becoming fluent in French, Italian and Spanish. Her first book, Celtic Road Home: A Memoir reflects upon her past adventures, while giving the reader a gentle, uplifting push to live out their very own life dreams. This follow-up book is a guide for all non-professional authors to live out a literary goal into becoming self-published.

Review and Thank You

If you have enjoyed reading this book, would you mind taking a few minutes to post a review on Amazon/Goodreads (as a Verified purchase)? It really does help with the book's algorithms. Thank you!

www.celticroadhome.com

HOW TO PROMOTE
That Book You Wrote
A Self-Publishing Guide

Happy Writing!

—Ann Doolan-Fox

www.ingramcontent.com/pod-product-compliance
Lightning Source LLC
Chambersburg PA
CBHW071852070526
44583CB00016B/1658